DATUM/DATE	NAAM/NAME	ADRES/ADDRESS	
23/1/03	Lila & Norman Lambert	Beer, Devon England	5* hope we may enjoy many more!
23/1/03	Verschueeegn Wilfried	Velbert Germany	Great Pleasure!
24/1 03	Rosemarie & Rdi Zülli	Hennef-Sieg GERMANY	Wir waren 2 Wochen hier es war eine sehr schöne Zeit. Danke!
24/1 03	Winnepoth Walter u. Ulla	Gidorf-Sieg Germany	2 wundervolle Wochen, wirklich ein service Danke!
25-1-2003	Peter & Douce Gallwey	Geneva Switzerland	what a lovely spot. Good food lovely welcoming Thank you -
25/1/03	Peter + Elizabeth Parr	Virginia Water UK	Great! Great! Great!
27/1/03	Connie en Jan Ciliacus	Hoeven Netherlands	10+ tops
	Schollbach Helfrich	Schwieberdingen Germany	Absolutely perfect

D'vine
restaurant
THE COOKBOOK

D'vine
restaurant
THE COOKBOOK

Gerald & Marc Hoberman

FEATURING THE CULINARY DELIGHTS AND INSIGHTS OF GOURMET CHEF
Loran Livesey

UNA PRESS, INC.
in association with
THE GERALD & MARC HOBERMAN COLLECTION
CAPE TOWN · LONDON · NEW YORK

To culinary inspiration and excellence.

DUNCAN SPENCE

Acknowledgements	7	*Starters*	23
Map	8	*Mains*	49
Introduction	11	*Desserts*	79
Q&A Loran Livesey, Anton Bekker & Ed Pearce	15	*Glossary*	107
		Index	109

Concept, photography, design and production control: Gerald and Marc Hoberman

Reproduction: Marc Hoberman
Text: Gerald Hoberman
Recipes: Loran Livesey
Layout: Jon Berndt
Editor: Roelien Theron
Indexer: Sandie Vahl
Cartographer: Peter Slingsby

www.hobermancollection.com

Copyright subsists in this material
Duplication by any means is prohibited without written permission from the copyright holder
Copyright © Gerald & Marc Hoberman 2003
First edition 2003

ISBN 0-9729822-2-1

D'vine Restaurant – The Cookbook is published by Una Press, Inc. in association with The Gerald & Marc Hoberman Collection (Pty) Ltd
Reg. No. 99/00167/07. PO Box 60044, Victoria Junction, 8005, Cape Town, South Africa
Telephone: 27-21-419 6657/419 2210 Fax: 27-21-418 5987 e-mail: office@hobermancollection.com

For copies of this book printed with your company's logo and corporate message contact The Gerald & Marc Hoberman Collection.

International marketing, corporate sales and picture library
Laurence Bard, Hoberman Collection (USA), Inc. / Una Press, Inc.
PO Box 880206, Boca Raton, FL 33488, USA
Telephone: (561) 542 1141 e-mail: hobcolus@bellsouth.net

Agents and distributors

United States of America, Canada and Asia	*Australia*	*Germany*	*Namibia*	*Republic of Ireland and Northern Ireland*	*United Kingdom*
BHB International, Inc.	Wakefield Press Distribution	Herold Verlagsauslieferung	Projects & Promotions cc	GSR Distributors Ltd.	DJ Segrue Ltd.
302 West North 2nd Street	Box 2266	& Logistik GmbH	PO Box 96102	47 Marley Court	7c Bourne Road
Seneca, SC 29678	Kent Town, SA 5071	Raiffeisenallee 10	Windhoek	Dublin 14	Bushey, Hertfordshire
Tel: (864) 885 9444	Tel: (0)8-8362 8800	82041 Oberhaching	Tel: (0)61-25 5715/6	Tel: (0)1-295 1205	WD23 3NH
Fax: (864) 885 1090	Fax: (0)8-8362 7592	Tel: (089) 61 38 710	Fax: (0)61-23 0033	Fax: (0)1-296 6403	Tel: (0)7976-273 225
bhbintl@bellsouth.net	sales@wakefieldpress.com.au	Fax: (089) 61 38 7120	proprom@iafrica.com.na	murray47@eircom.net	Fax: (0)20-8421 9577
		herold@herold-va.de			sales@djsegrue.co.uk

Printed in Singapore

Acknowledgements

We were invited to create a book that reflects the excellence and ambience of D'vine Restaurant in Somerset West and the extraordinary cooking of its gourmet chef Loran Livesey. Loran's quietly authoritative command and unflappable manner and the dedicated cooperation of her kitchen staff enabled us to photograph each dish naturally as it is served at the table. Loran's understanding, whenever a dish was returned from a shoot empty, was much appreciated.

We are most appreciative, too, of the invaluable contributions of general managers Anton Bekker and Ed Pearce, charming hosts who go to great lengths to anticipate and cater to their guests' every whim.

In addition, we are grateful to all those people listed below who also made a meaningful contribution to the book.

GERALD & MARC HOBERMAN

Claudine Apollis
Julio Bertram, Morgenster Olive Farm
Sandy Bailey
Hanneke du Toit
Bollie Ganief
Samantha Hardie
Hazel Hoberman

Brian Kirsch
Pearl Mbana
Manny Mendelsohn
Rebecca Nkoana
Michael Snyman
Martilie Vosloo
Kobus Weyers

D'vine Restaurant

AT WILLOWBROOK LODGE, SOMERSET WEST
50 KILOMETRES FROM CAPE TOWN ON THE N2, EXIT 43

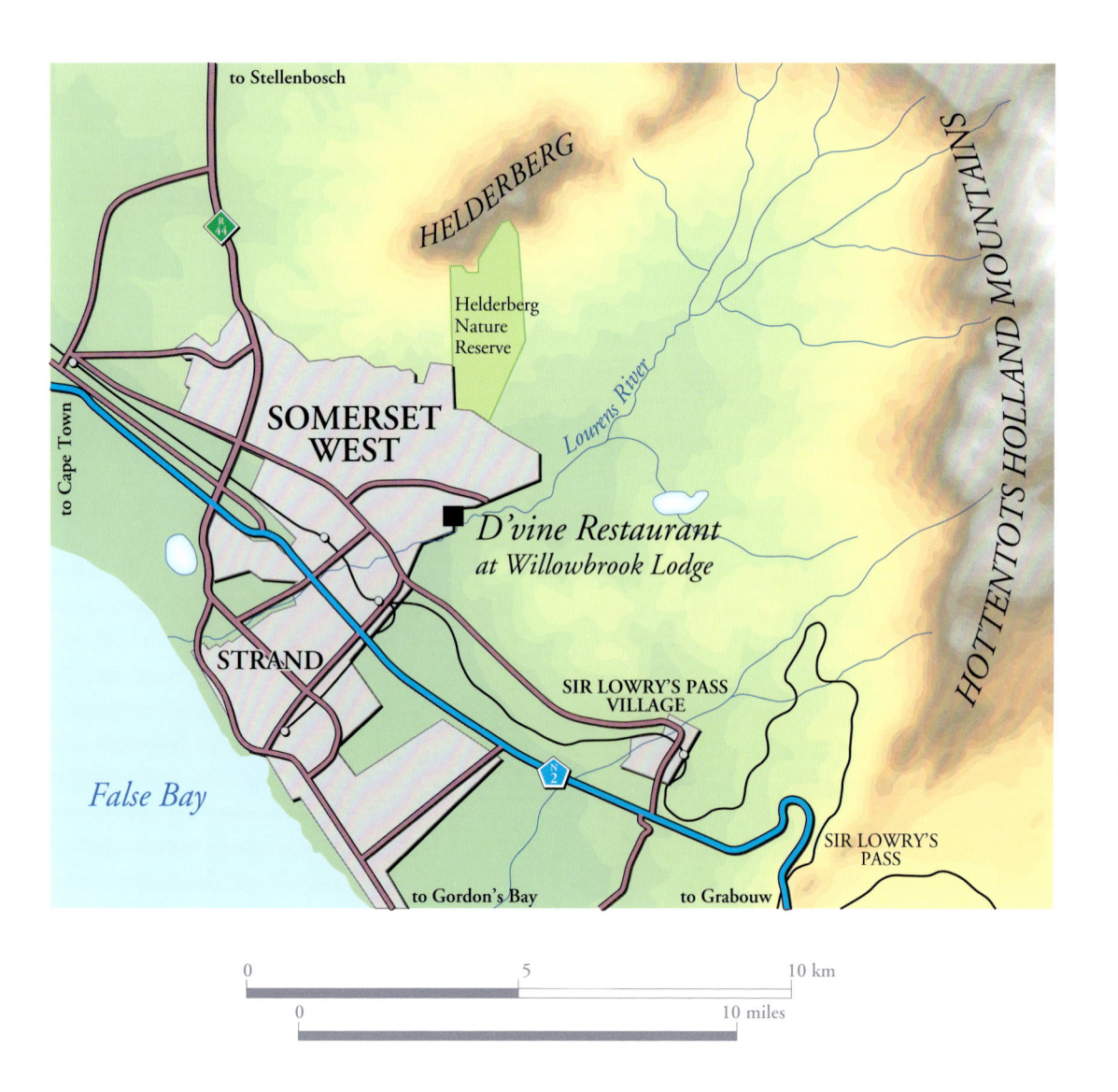

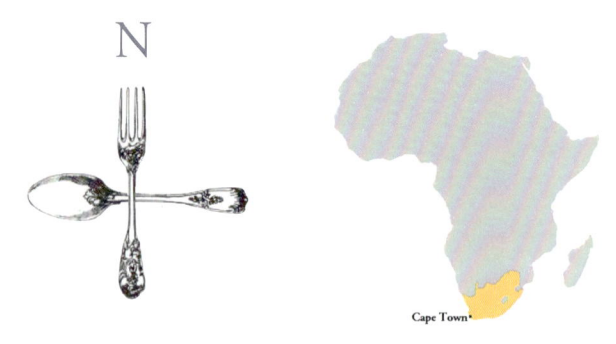

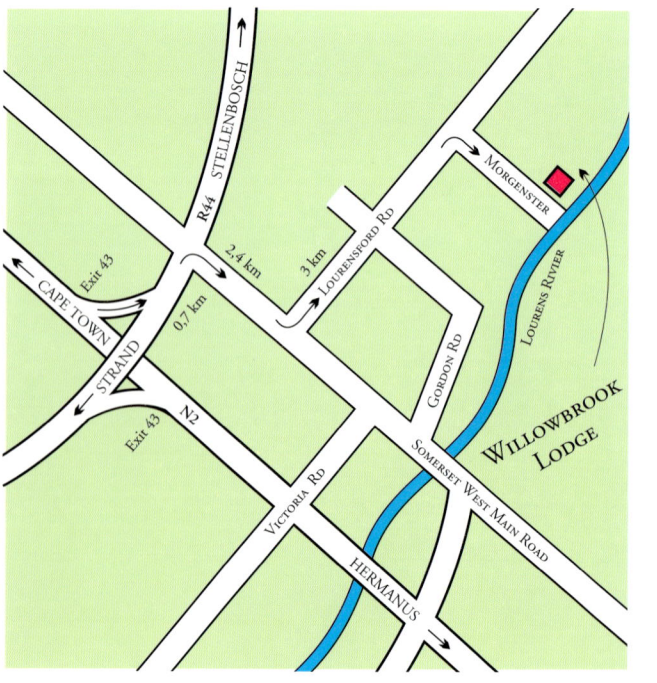

Loran Livesey, executive chef, D'vine Restaurant.

The kitchen door of D'vine Restaurant.

Introduction

A growing international reputation for culinary excellence and an atmosphere of tranquillity and sparkling hospitality have made D'vine Restaurant at Willowbrook Lodge in Somerset West an important stopover for visitors to South Africa. Situated in the heart of the Cape winelands on the famous Cape Wine Route, D'vine Restaurant is a memorable pause in the vivid, vibrant symphony of what has become known as the 'African experience'.

Somerset West, named after Lord Charles Somerset, the British governor at the Cape from 1814 to 1820, offers sophisticated country living. Here, amid montane splendour and the pristine beaches of the nearby Strand, the sun-drenched grape vines of the Cape are cooled by gentle sea breezes – ideal conditions for the creation of its excellent wines.

It is in this beautiful village that we were inspired to provide, through this book, a window to the kitchen of executive chef Loran Livesey. In *D'vine Restaurant – The Cookbook*, Loran has opened her kitchen and her heart to share her world, her celebrated recipes, her unique approach to fine dining and her various presentation styles with you. The gastronomic experience provided by this exceptional restaurant is highlighted by the impeccable attention to detail of hosts Anton Bekker and Ed Pearce who treat their guests with a warmth that reflects both the glorious African sunshine and an old world hospitality.

The recipes selected for this book are firm favourites of those sophisticated and discerning international diners who fill Loran's restaurant day and night. Her epicurean masterpieces should inspire both gourmet cooks and novices to venture into their own kitchens, spatulas at the ready, to try the easy-to-follow recipes in this collection. Those lucky enough to have experienced Loran's cooking at its finest will find this cookbook a fitting memento of their visit to D'vine Restaurant.

Bon appétit or, as we say in Africa, 'born up a tree'!

GERALD & MARC HOBERMAN
Somerset West

Anybody can make you enjoy the first bite of a dish, but only a real chef can make you enjoy the last.

FRANÇOIS MINOT, EDITOR OF *GUIDE MICHELIN*

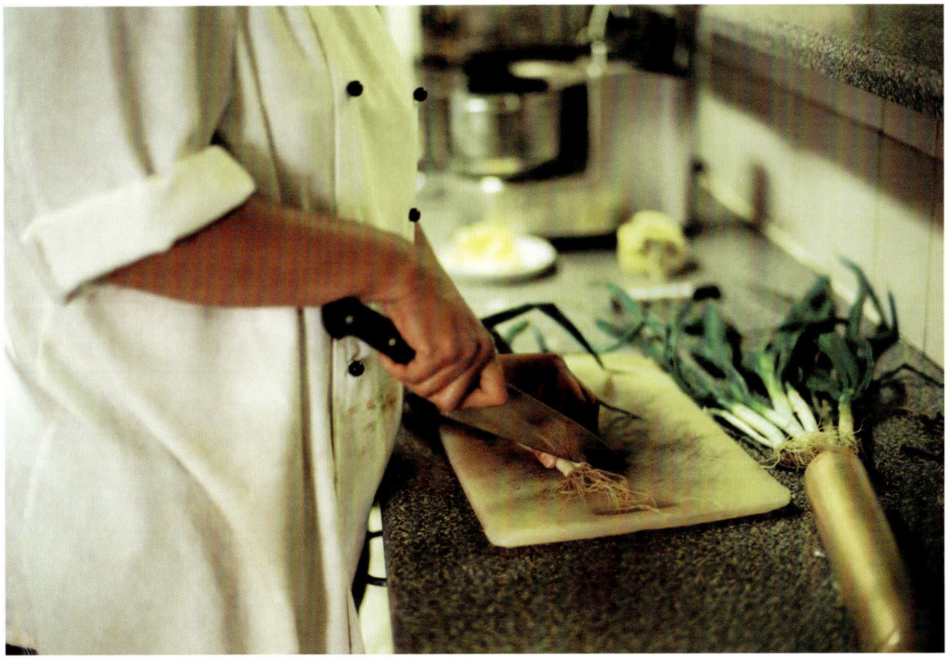

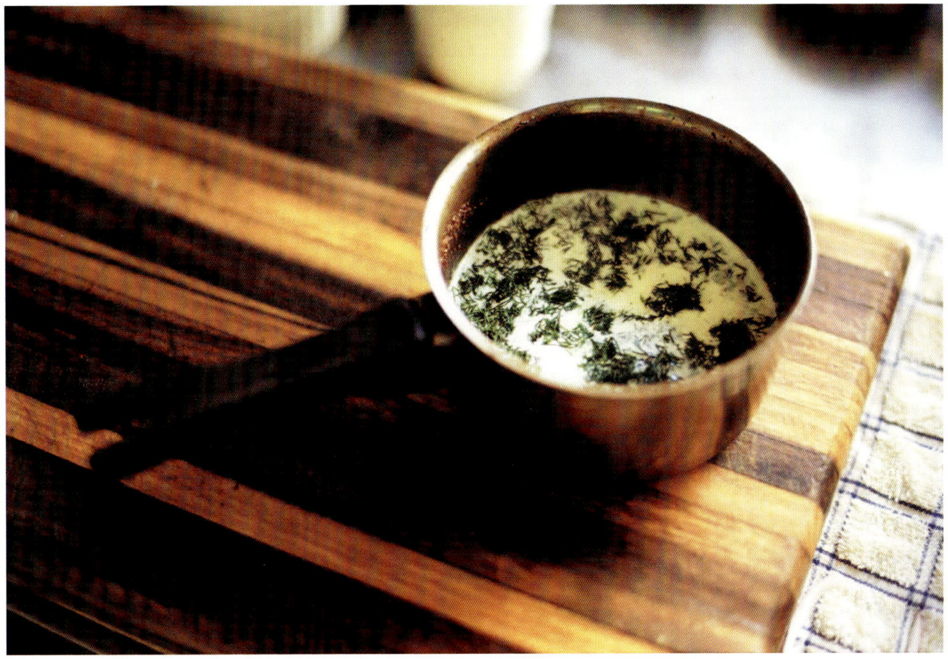

LORAN LIVESEY – EXECUTIVE CHEF, D'VINE RESTAURANT

Executive chef Loran Livesey is the captain of her kitchen. Cook extraordinaire, food stylist and a perfectionist who pays meticulous attention to detail, she runs a tight ship in the famous D'vine Restaurant at Willowbrook Lodge.

This charming yet unassuming chef has attracted a loyal following of discerning international diners who rave about her culinary skills. The comments recorded in the visitors' book reflect the high regard in which she is held.

Loran was born in Durban in KwaZulu-Natal and educated at Franschhoek High School in the renowned Cape winelands. She trained at the highly respected Silwood Kitchen Cordons Bleus School of Cookery in Cape Town under the watchful eye of the late Lesley Faull. Her three-year education in the culinary arts included practical training at Burgundy Restaurant in Hermanus near Cape Town and at Willowbrook Lodge where, under the supervision of Joanne van Staden, she worked with famous French chefs Didier Lailheugue and Alexandre Coupy. She rounded off her cooking education at the two-star Michelin hotel and restaurant Prinses Juliana in Valkenburg, Holland. In 2000 she became executive chef at the Willowbrook Lodge restaurant, later renamed D'vine Restaurant. Willowbrook general manager Ed Pearce describes her food as 'local with a twist and a special international flair'.

Q & A

Gerald and Marc Hoberman speak to executive chef Loran Livesey and general managers of D'vine Restaurant Anton Bekker and Ed Pearce

Who has had the most influence on your cooking career?
Loran: Undoubtedly Joanne van Staden played a great role in my development as a cook. Although she was a tough mentor, she was both a strong influence and an inspiration to me.

What are your favourite dishes?
Loran: For starters, I'd select foie gras, followed by a main course of truffles and other wild mushrooms. My favourite dessert is frozen berry parfait served with hot blackberries flambéed at the table.

How do you present your food?
Loran: I prefer delicate yet ample portions. I like to create a simple but eye-catching feast for the palate and for the eye. Before the plates are taken to the table, I decorate them with, for example, turmeric, paprika or berry coulis. It's my way of producing a work of art for our guests.

How do you choose your ingredients?
Loran: I use a great variety of fresh ingredients, and my dishes reflect seasonal variations. I also have a special relationship with my suppliers who often go that extra mile in bringing me superior produce. I always exercise careful control over quality and size.

Norwegian salmon, duck magret (duck breast) and mozzarella cheese are flown in weekly from Europe. The duck is rich in colour, has a more concentrated flavour than local duck, and is particularly tender. The ingredients for the wild mushroom terrine on our menu are imported from France.

We have freshwater crawfish on our menu. It is an unusual dish, served thermidor style or *en papillote* (in phyllo pastry). I personally go crayfish diving on occasion. Fresh fish is bought straight from the fishermen at the Strand jetty. Most of our oysters come from the West Coast.

I use a wide range of fresh berries from Stellenbosch. These include blueberries, blackberries, raspberries, tayberries, mulberries and Cape gooseberries.

We bake our own bread and make our own preserves, jam, ice cream, sorbet, atjar and chutney.

Other special ingredients include the flowers of courgette plants which we grow at Willowbrook Lodge. They bloom around Valentine's Day and are filled with ham and pine kernels to create a unique and romantic dish.

Do you ever get 'heated' in the kitchen?
Loran: Occasionally.

You are famous for your superb sauces. Tell us about them.
Loran: My sauces are made from scratch. I always begin by making my own stock from animal bones and then reducing the mixture to a thick consistency. Cold butter is whisked in at the end. Meat sauces are never thickened with flour.

Do you ever cook when you're off duty?
Loran: I like to cook for my family, but I also love going to other restaurants and being served.

Tell us a bit about your kitchen staff and your waiters and waitresses.
Loran: I have a happy and motivated staff. Some of them started out as scullery hands and have thrived on being trained with a generosity of spirit in a cool, calm environment.

What are your favourite utensils?
Loran: A good sharp knife and my slicer, smoker and *dim sum* baskets.

Are you daring and innovative in the kitchen?
Loran: Yes, I am. Some of my most innovative dishes are fresh fig carpaccio; pear and fennel bulb soup; and tomato and nectarine soup. I enjoy presenting two or three different soups in one dish, garnished with deep-fried herbs.

How would you describe your cooking style?
Loran: I am comfortable focusing on French cuisine complemented by international dishes. My menus include springbok, ostrich and other local game, as well as curries and vegetarian fare. The management has given me *carte blanche* to devise inventive and original dishes, and I'm encouraged to add my own personal signature to each dish.

What are your plans for the future of D'vine Restaurant?
Loran: I want it to become the finest restaurant in South Africa, booked out months in advance!

Ed Pearce, Loran Livesey, Pearl Mbana and Anton Bekker.

How would you describe D'vine Restaurant at Willowbrook Lodge?
Anton & Ed: It offers a unique gastronomic experience. The ambience is congenial and elegant, yet informal – friendly, personal attention is lavished on each guest. Dining is unhurried, as we take single bookings only. D'vine Restaurant is definitely a place to say you've been to and not just seen.

You appear to greet guests with a sparkle in your eyes and a spring in your step. How do you do it?
Anton & Ed: We genuinely love receiving our guests. We try to be well-ironed without the starch! We love a little bit of banter spiced with humour. People often come as guests and leave as friends, returning time and again thereafter to re-experience the charm and culinary delights of the lodge and restaurant. The place exudes the intangible qualities of serenity and tranquillity. People are at peace here.

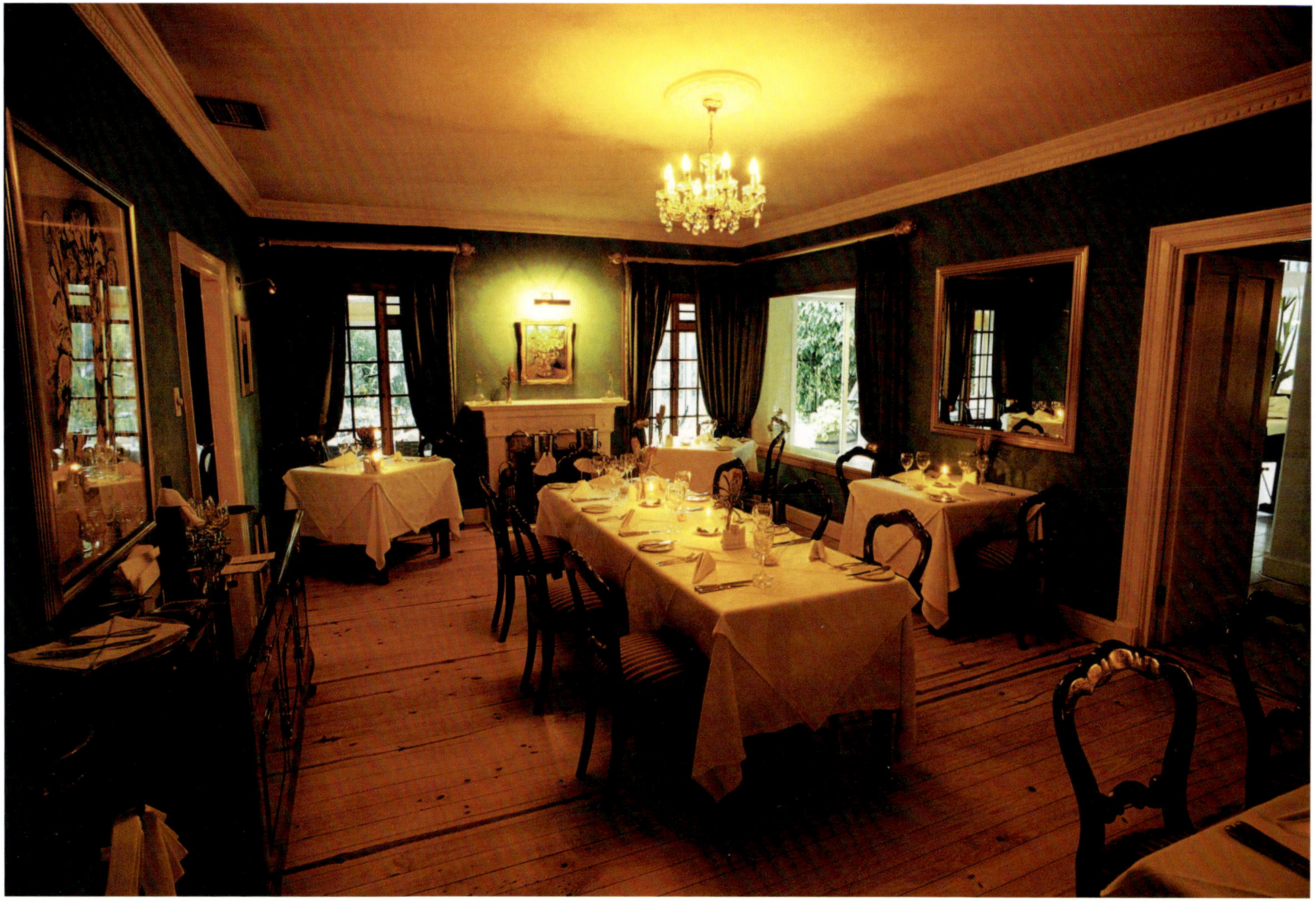

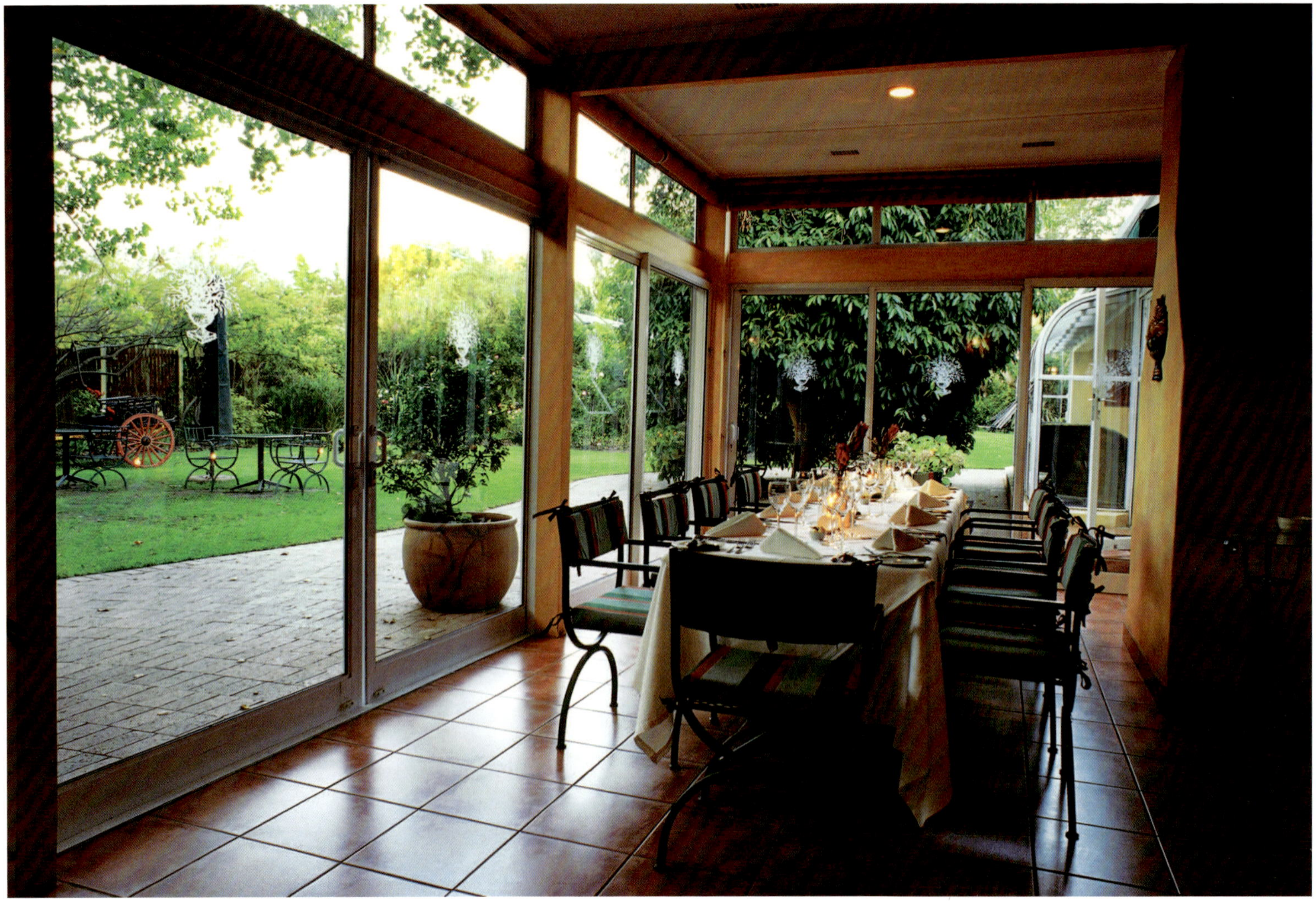

The attentive staff of D'vine Restaurant at Willowbrook Lodge (from left to right): Ed Pearce, Pearl Mbana and Anton Bekker.

WILLOWBROOK
Lodge

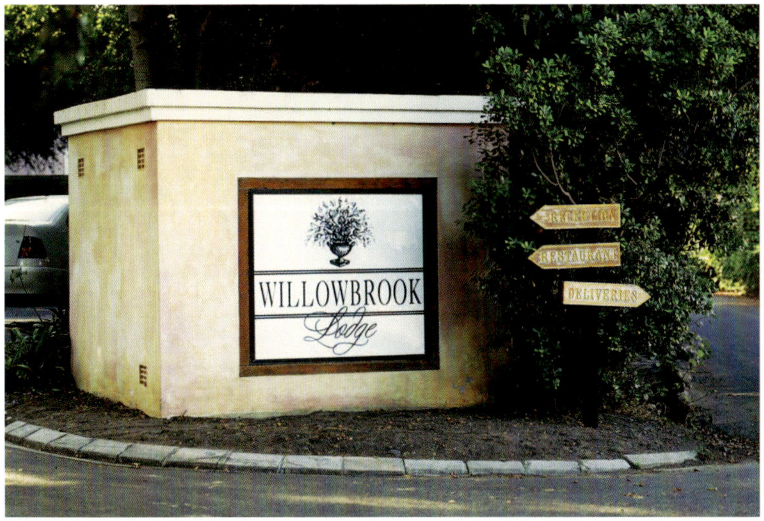
WILLOWBROOK
Lodge
RESTAURANT
DELIVERIES

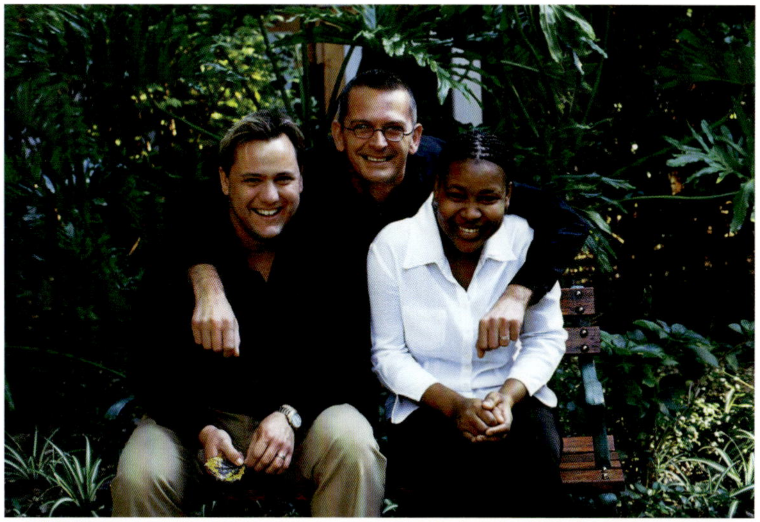

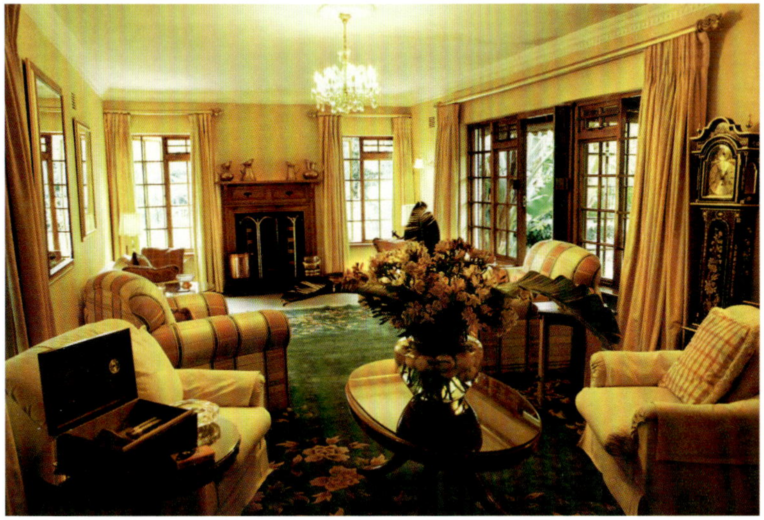

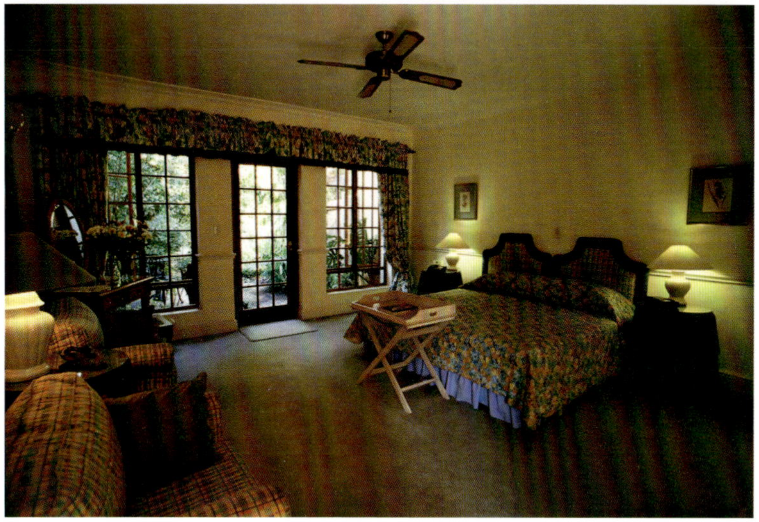

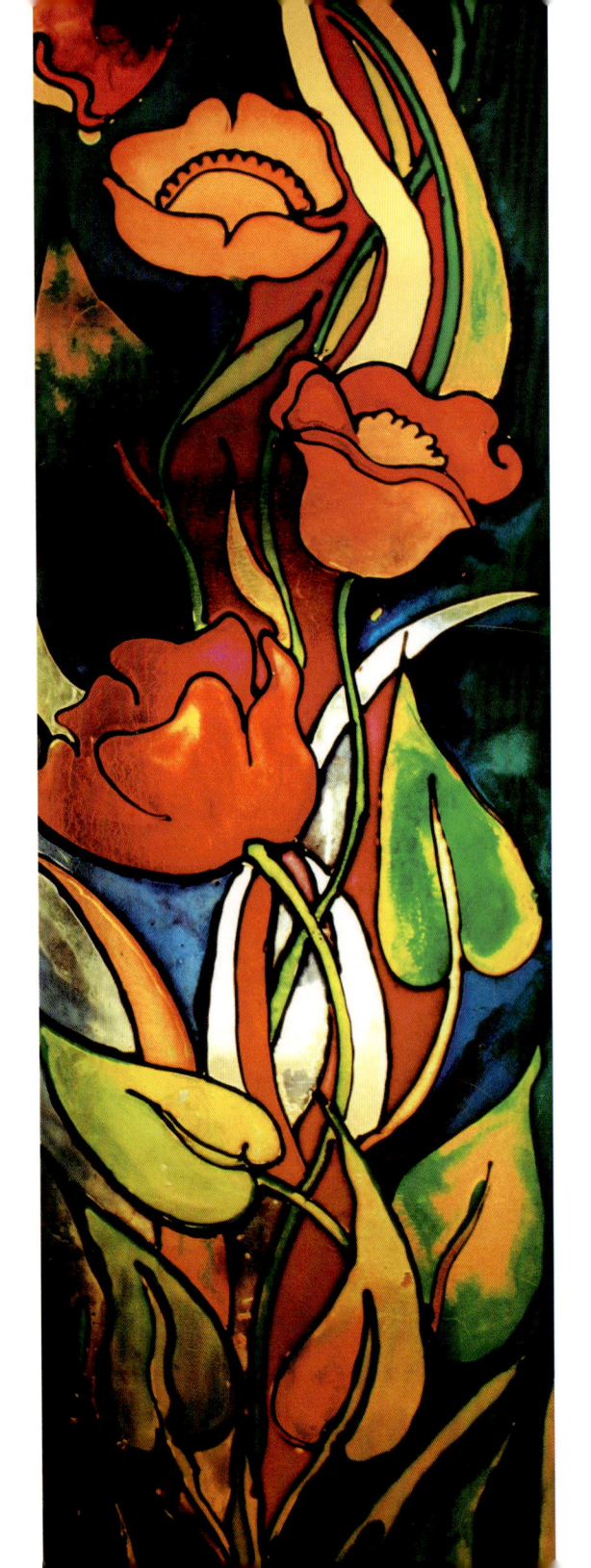

Food responds to our soul's dream as to our stomach's appetite.

Joseph Delteil (1894–1978), author of *La Cuisine Paléolithique* (1964)

Starters

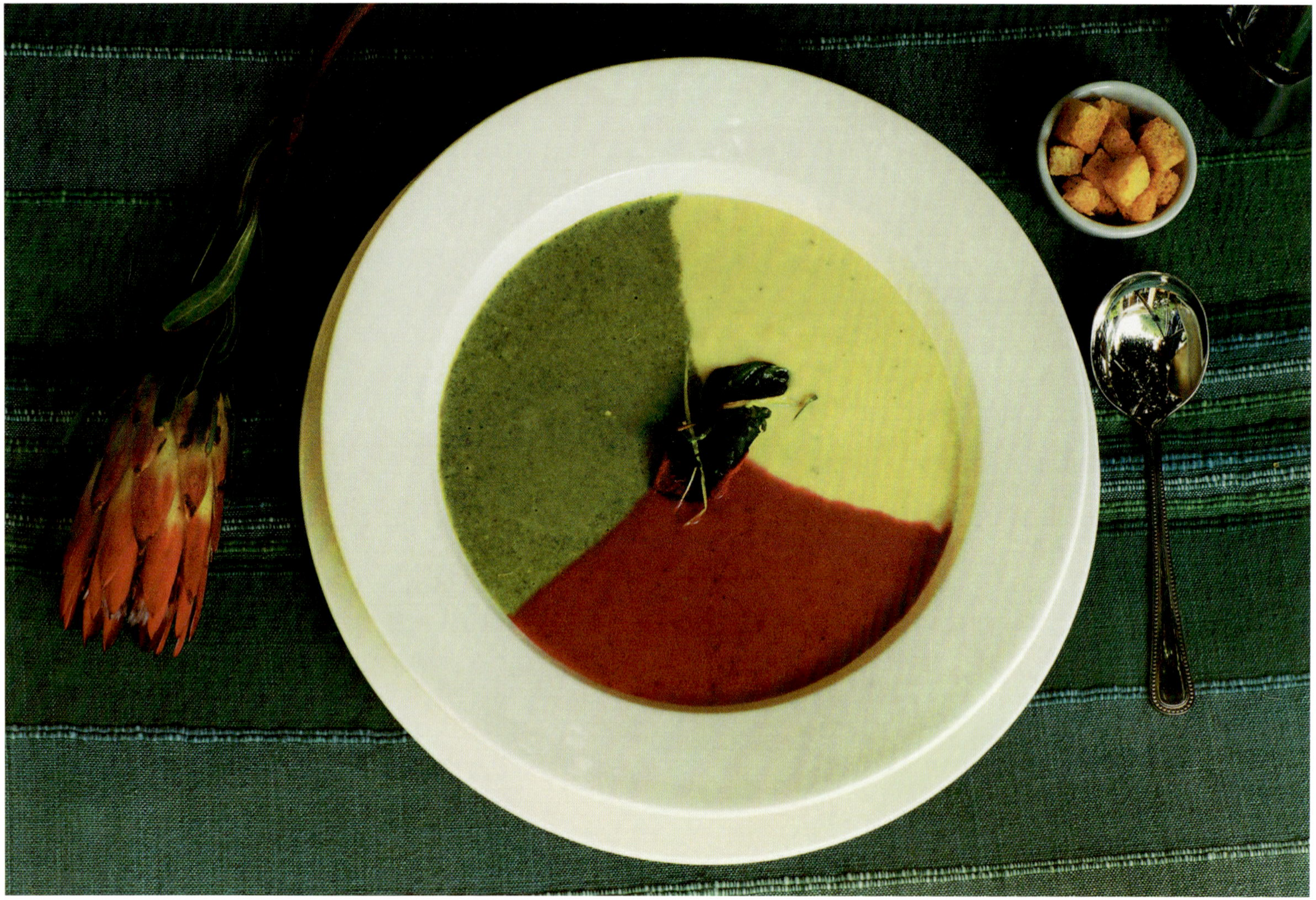

Serves 4

Beetroot soup

10 g butter
1 onion, finely chopped
1 clove garlic, crushed
1 potato, diced
400 g beetroot, roughly chopped
250 ml cream
1 litre chicken or vegetable stock
45 ml fresh thyme
salt & pepper

Leek and potato soup

10 g butter
1 onion, finely chopped
1 clove garlic, crushed
1 potato, diced
400 g leeks, thinly sliced
250 ml cream
1 litre chicken or vegetable stock
45 ml fresh thyme
salt & pepper

Broccoli soup

10 g butter
1 onion, finely chopped
1 clove garlic, crushed
1 potato, diced
400 g broccoli florets
250 ml cream
1 litre chicken or vegetable stock
45 ml fresh thyme
salt & pepper

Trio of Soup

Beetroot soup

Heat the butter in a saucepan. Add the onion, garlic, potato and beetroot and sauté for approximately 5 minutes over a medium heat. Reduce the heat, then add the cream, stock, thyme, salt and pepper. Simmer for 45 minutes. Season to taste. When cool, blend the mixture in a blender. Strain and return the soup to the saucepan. Keep warm until needed.

Leek and potato soup

Heat the butter in a saucepan. Add the onion, garlic, potato and leeks and sauté for approximately 5 minutes over a medium heat. Reduce the heat, then add the cream, stock, thyme, salt and pepper. Simmer for 45 minutes. Season to taste. When cool, blend the mixture in a blender. Strain and return the soup to the saucepan. Keep warm until needed.

Broccoli soup

Heat the butter in a saucepan. Add the onion, garlic, potato and broccoli and sauté for approximately 5 minutes over a medium heat. Reduce the heat, then add the cream, stock, thyme, salt and pepper. Simmer for 45 minutes. Season to taste. When cool, blend the mixture in a blender. Strain and return the soup to the saucepan. Keep warm until needed.

When ready to serve, gently heat the three soup mixtures. With the help of an extra pair of hands, use 3 jugs to carefully pour the 3 soups simultaneously into the soup bowls.

Serve with thin slices of toasted ciabatta or French baguette covered with herb butter.

Suggested wine: Chenin Blanc

Serves 4

200 g coarse salt
50 g coarse black pepper
50 g sugar
200 g Norwegian salmon
salt and pepper to taste
beluga caviar for garnish
quail eggs for garnish

Salsa

45 ml extra virgin olive oil
1 large aubergine, chopped
2 shallots, finely chopped
10 ml sherry vinegar
3 ml ground cumin
4 cardamom pods, crushed
5 ml garam masala
1 large pickled gherkin, chopped
10 ml fresh coriander, chopped
10 ml fresh basil leaves, chopped
2 chives, chopped
salt & pepper to taste

Smoked Salmon and Aubergine Salsa

Prepare the salmon by mixing the salt, pepper and sugar together. Place the salmon (skin side down) in a dish and cover the top of the fish with the mixture. Cover the dish and leave it in the fridge for 1 hour. The salt will draw liquid from the salmon, keeping it moist.

Remove the dish from the refrigerator and wash the salt marinade off the salmon. Smoke the salmon for 10 minutes (see below). Cool, cover and refrigerate until needed.

To make the salsa, heat 30 ml of the oil in a heavy-based pan. Add the aubergine and shallots and cook over a low heat until the aubergine is soft. Add the vinegar, spices and gherkin. Remove from the heat and pour the mixture into a bowl. Mix in the chopped herbs and remaining oil. Season with salt and pepper.

Cover the salsa with cling film and let it stand until cold for flavours to infuse. Do not refrigerate the mixture while still hot.

Adjust seasoning if necessary.

When ready to serve, slice the salmon finely. Serve with aubergine salsa and garnish with poached quail eggs and beluga caviar.

Home smoking

Use a roasting dish (30 cm x 20 cm) with a lid. Place 2 cups of oak wood shavings on the bottom of the dish. Oak wood shavings can be obtained from a hardware store. Place the salmon on a raised cooling rack (used for cooling cakes and pastries) on top of the shavings. Make sure that there is no contact between the fish and the wood shavings, otherwise the fish will taste bitter. Cover the dish with a lid and smoke over a very low heat on a hob or hot stove plate. When removing the lid, be careful of the escaping smoke. Ensure that the room in which you are smoking the fish is well ventilated.

Suggested wine: Chardonnay or Semillon

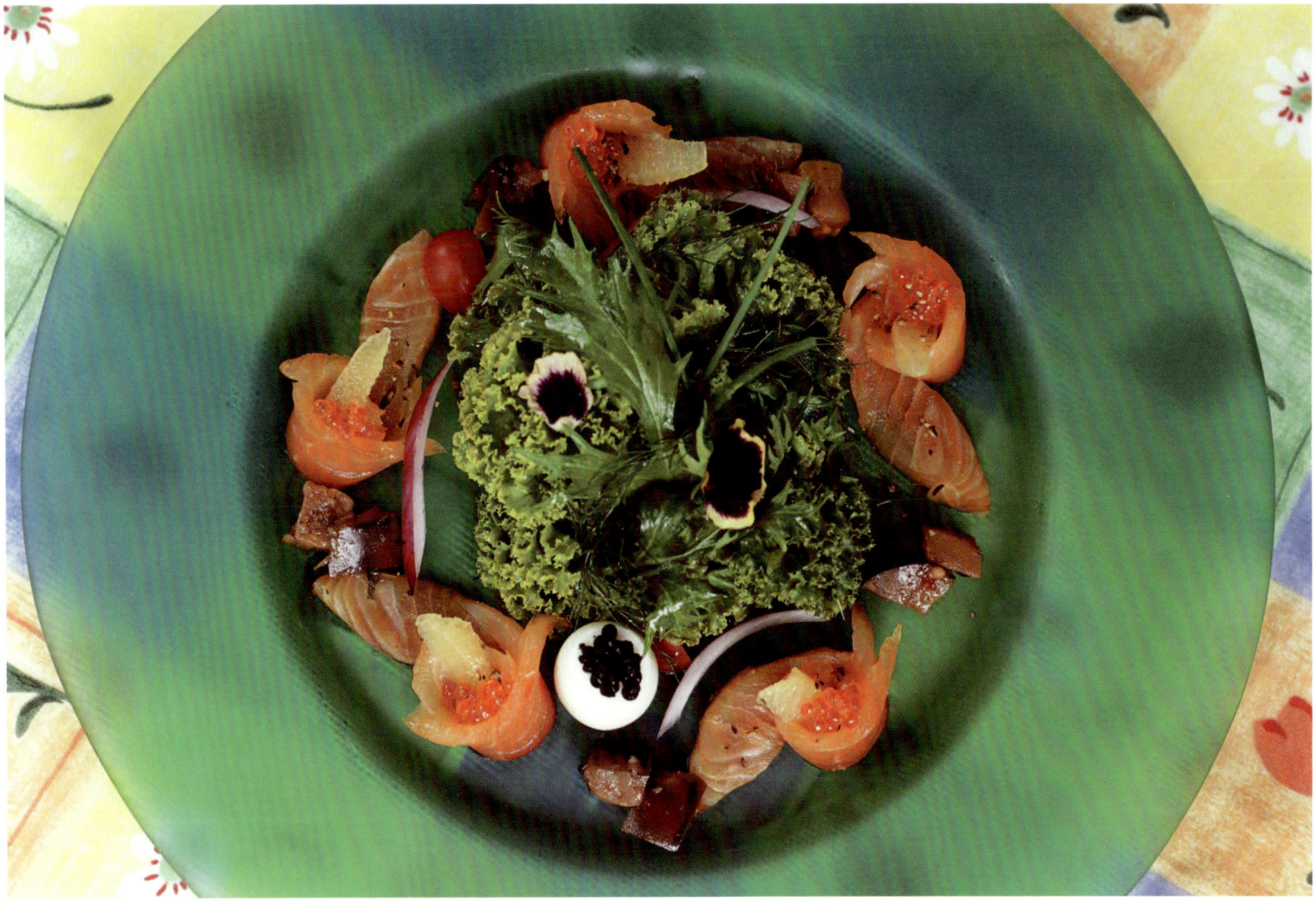

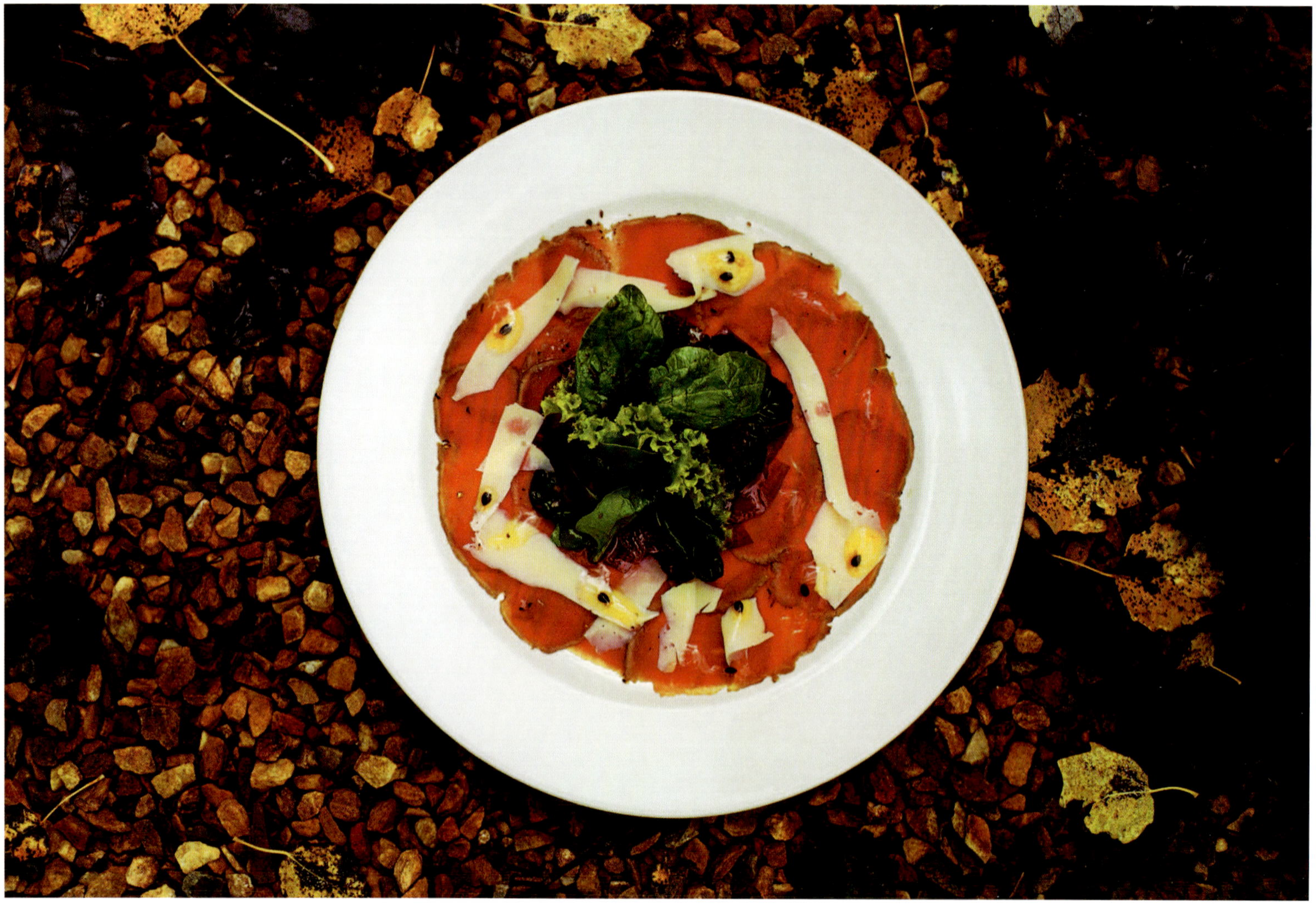

Serves 4

150 g kudu fillet
5 ml dried mixed herbs
salt & pepper to taste
125 ml raspberry vinegar
100 ml grapeseed oil
1 clove garlic, crushed
1 raw beetroot, peeled
50 ml Parmesan cheese shavings
2 passionfruit

Raspberry vinaigrette

100 ml raspberry vinegar
100 ml extra virgin olive oil
5 ml fresh thyme, chopped
2 ml English mustard
salt & pepper to taste

Beetroot and Kudu Carpaccio with Raspberry Vinaigrette

Coat the kudu fillet with the mixed herbs, salt and pepper. Fry the fillet for 4 minutes on each side. To make a marinade, mix together the raspberry vinegar, grapeseed oil and garlic. Marinate the fillet in the mixture for 6 hours and keep refrigerated during this time. Remove the kudu from the marinade and cover it in tin foil. Place the fillet in a freezer until frozen and ready to use.

When ready to serve, cut the frozen kudu and beetroot into very thin slices and arrange on a serving plate.

To make the raspberry vinaigrette, combine all the ingredients in a food processor and blend until smooth. Drizzle the vinaigrette over the kudu and beetroot slices.

Garnish with Parmesan cheese shavings, passionfruit pulp and black pepper.

Suggested wine: Cabernet or Pinotage

Serves 4

coarse sea salt
4 medium beetroot, whole
140 g soft goat cheese
60 ml extra virgin olive oil
5 ml fresh chives, chopped
5 ml marjoram, chopped
salt & pepper to taste
50 g walnuts

Beetroot chips

1 whole peeled beetroot
vegetable oil

Beetroot sauce

1 whole peeled beetroot
100 g sugar
250 ml raspberry vinegar

Beetroot, Goat Cheese and Walnut Galette

Preheat the oven to 180 °C.

Cover the bottom of a roasting pan with coarse salt. Arrange the beetroot on top of the salt and roast them for 40 minutes until soft. Remove the beetroot from the salt base. Peel the beetroot and cut each one horizontally into 4 slices.

In a bowl, mix the goat cheese, olive oil, herbs, salt and pepper until smooth.

To make the beetroot chips, thinly slice 1 beetroot using a slicer. Deep-fry the beetroot slices in vegetable oil. Drain the chips on towelling paper.

Prepare the beetroot sauce by boiling the beetroot in a pot of water. Make sure the water covers the beetroot. When the beetroot is soft, strain the mixture. Remove the beetroot, chop roughly and then blend it in a food processor until smooth. Strain through a fine sieve. Return the strained mixture to the pot and add the sugar and raspberry vinegar. Reduce the mixture over a high heat until a thick consistency is achieved.

To assemble, arrange alternate layers of the beetroot slices and the goat cheese blend, finishing with the cheese. Top with walnuts and beetroot chips. Spoon the beetroot sauce attractively around the galette.

Suggested wine: Chardonnay

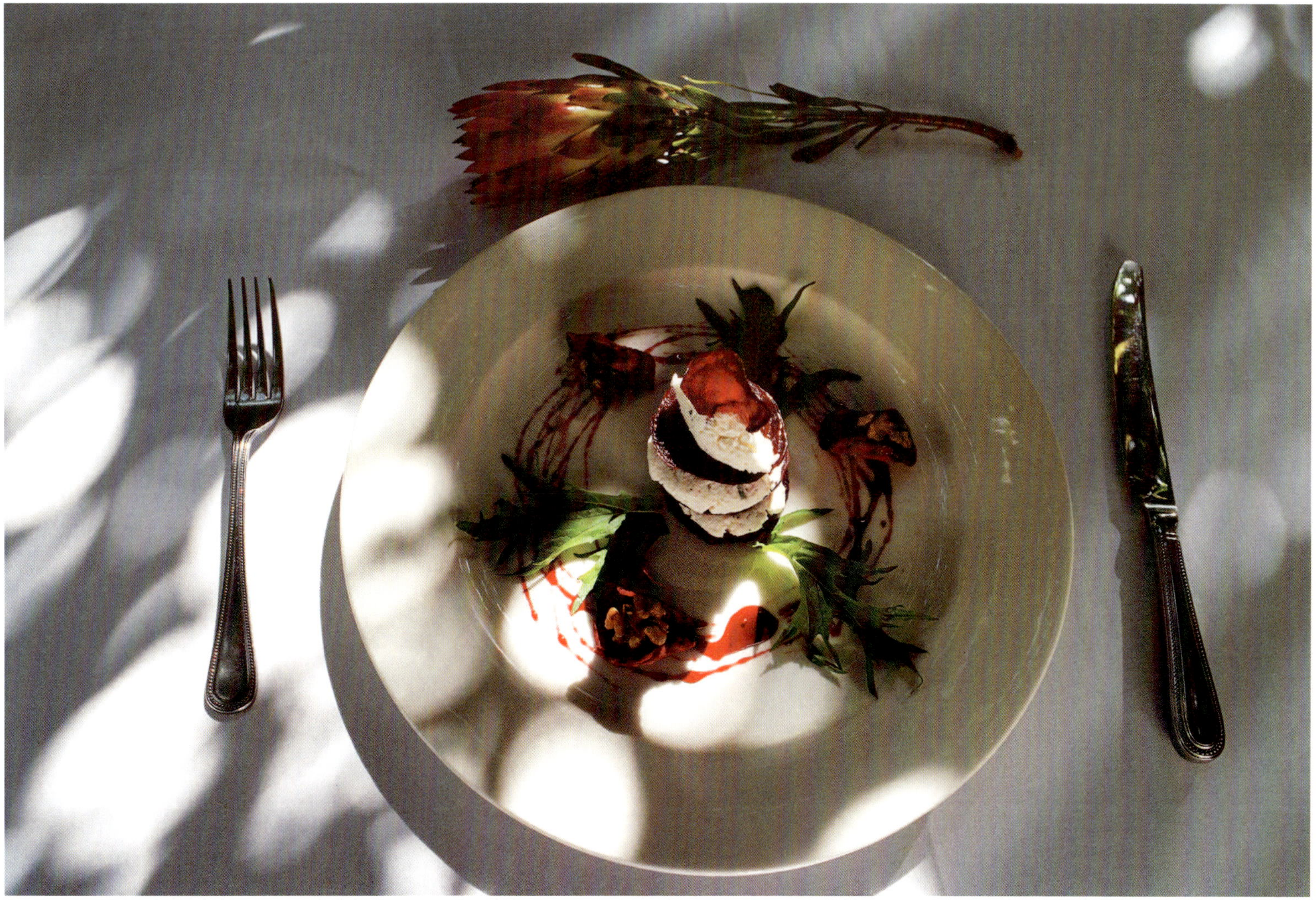

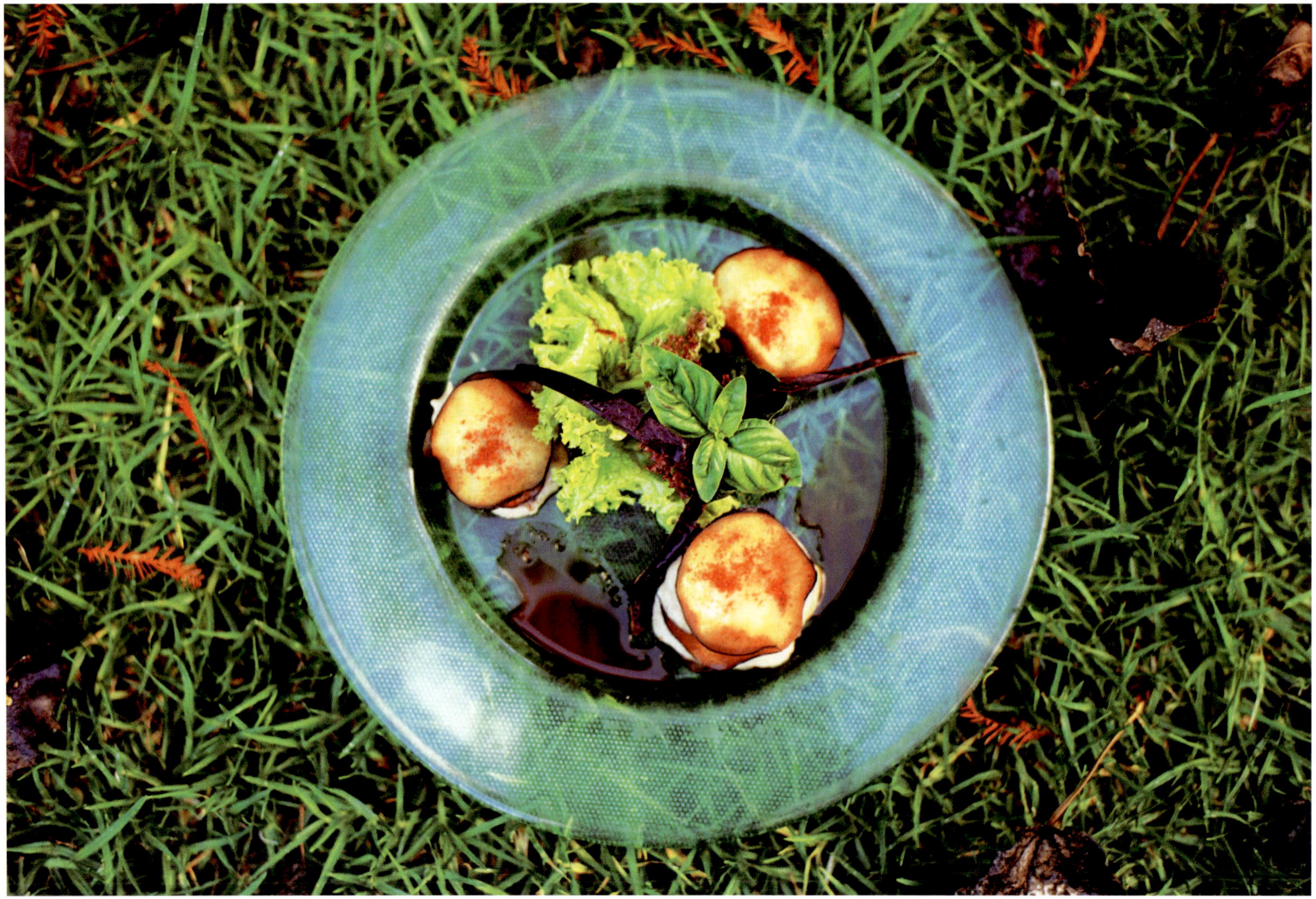

Timbale of Aubergine

Serves 4

6 large aubergines
125 ml extra virgin olive oil
2 cloves garlic, crushed
salt
5 ml cumin seeds
6 cardamom pods, crushed
juice of 3 lemons
50 ml chives, chopped
vegetable oil
edible flowers (for example, nasturtiums, chive flowers, pineapple sage flowers)

Preheat the oven to 200 °C.

Mix together 10 ml olive oil, garlic and salt and coat 4 aubergines with the mixture. Roast the aubergines whole in the oven for 60 minutes until soft. Cut the aubergines in half and remove the flesh.

To make the aubergine caviar, crush the cumin seeds and cardamom pods using a mortar and pestle. Mix the crushed spices with the aubergine flesh. Slowly add the lemon juice and remaining olive oil. Season to taste and add the chives. Set aside to cool. Cover the aubergine caviar and refrigerate until needed.

Cut the remaining aubergines into thin rounds with a slicer or a very sharp knife, and deep-fry them in the vegetable oil. Drain the excess oil, using towelling paper.

To assemble the timbale, scoop a layer of the aubergine caviar onto a plate and top it with an aubergine chip. Arrange in alternate layers until 4 layers have been created.

Garnish with chives and edible flowers.

Suggested wine: Sauvignon Blanc

Serves 4

1 green pepper
1 red pepper
1 yellow pepper
4 large courgettes, sliced lengthwise
4 yellow patty pan squashes, sliced lengthwise
1 large aubergine, sliced thinly
15 ml extra virgin olive oil
2 garlic cloves, chopped
20 ml fresh thyme, chopped
250 g goat cheese
salt & pepper to taste

Puff pastry sticks

puff pastry
tapenade (page 107)

Vegetable Terrine

Preheat the oven grill.

Halve the peppers and remove the seeds and stems. Place the peppers, courgettes, patty pans and aubergine on a baking tray. Sprinkle the vegetables with half of the chopped garlic and thyme. Brush the vegetables lightly with the oil and grill for approximately 2 minutes on each side.

In a bowl, mix the remaining garlic and thyme with the goat cheese.

Line a bread tin with cling film. Line the bottom of the tin with the courgettes. Alternate the layers of vegetables according to their colours and separate each layer with a layer of the goat cheese mixture.

Cover the bread tin with cling film. Compress the terrine by covering the tin with a piece of cardboard and placing a weight (about 1 kg) on top of the cardboard. Place in the fridge for 6 hours.

Meanwhile, prepare the puff pastry sticks. Slice the puff pastry into 8 strips, about 1 cm wide. Baste the strips with the tapenade and twist. Bake the sticks in the oven for 10 minutes at 180 °C until golden brown.

To serve, remove the terrine from the bread tin and unwrap the cling film. Slice and serve 2 slices per portion.

Serve with puff pastry sticks and a salad of your choice.

Suggested wine: Chenin Blanc

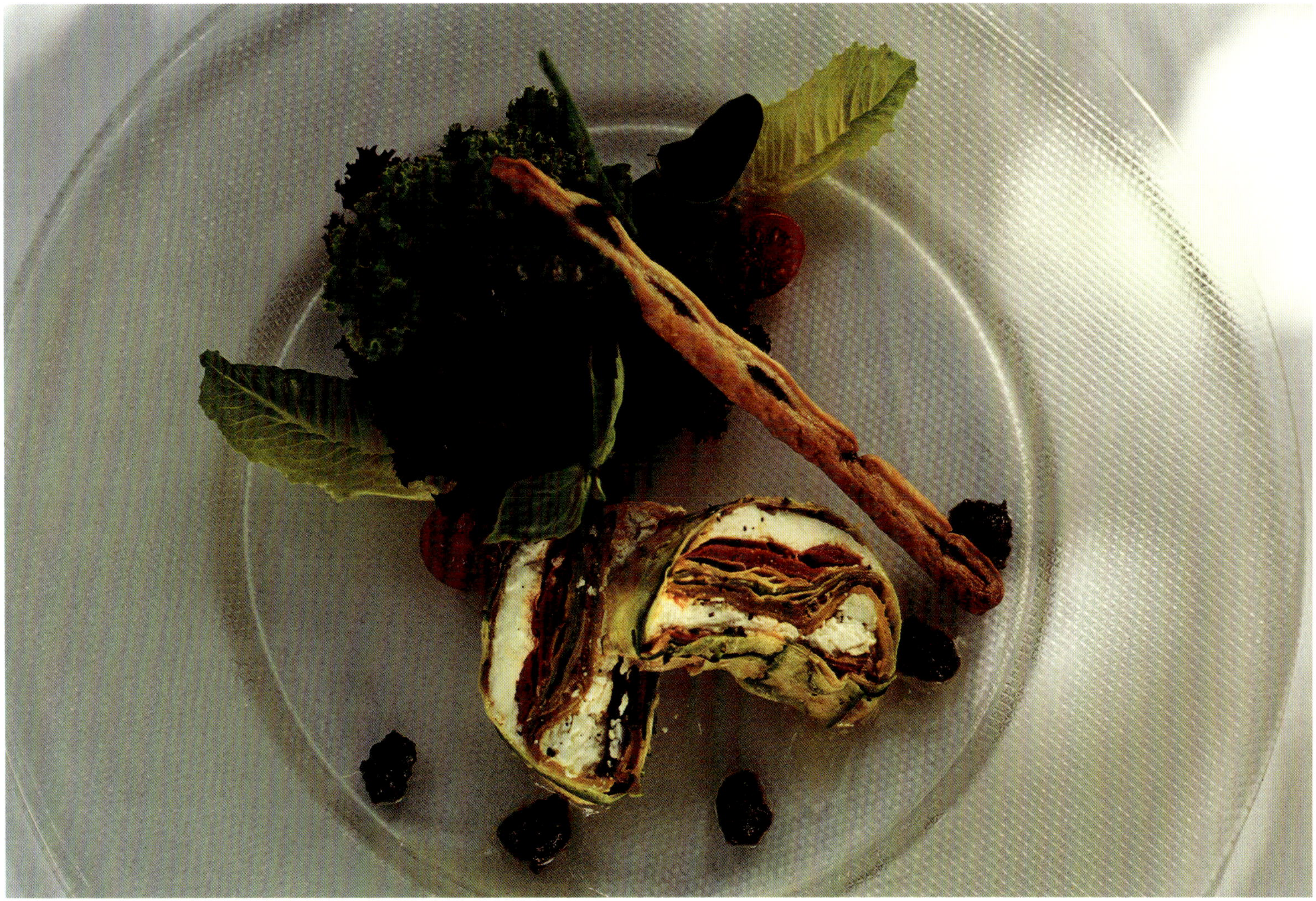

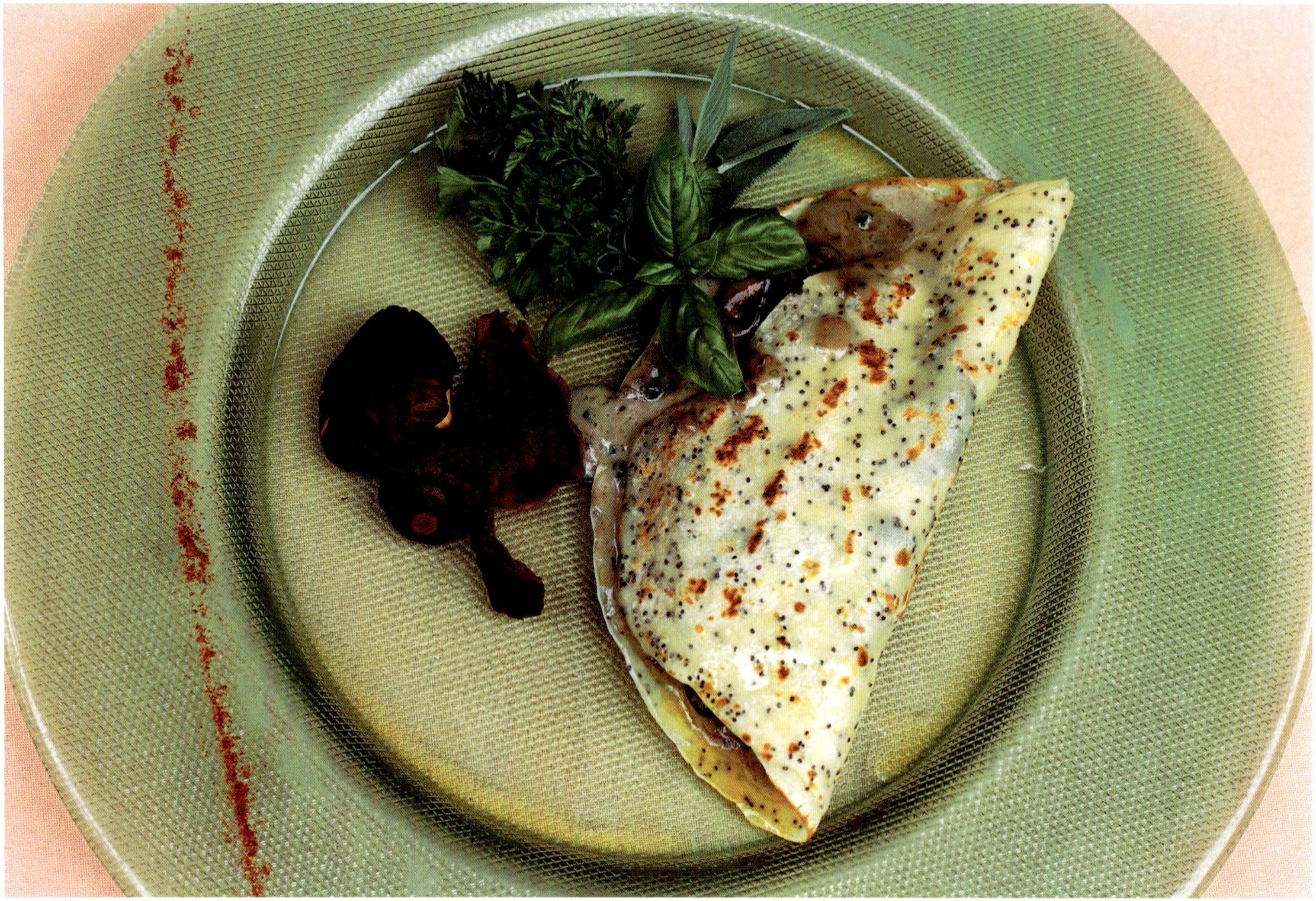

Wild Mushroom Crêpe

Serves 4

110 g cake flour
300 ml full cream milk
2 eggs
15 ml vegetable oil
pinch of salt
10 ml poppy seeds

Wild mushroom filling

700 g mixed wild mushrooms (available in speciality stores)
5 ml extra virgin olive oil
1 small onion, sliced
1 clove garlic, crushed
15 ml fresh basil, chopped
15 ml fresh tarragon, chopped
10 ml chives, chopped
500 ml thick cream
truffle oil for garnish
Parmesan cheese for garnish

Sift the flour into a bowl. Make a well in the centre and add the milk, eggs, oil and salt. Gradually mix until smooth. Stir in the poppy seeds.

Cover the bottom of a crêpe pan with a thin layer of vegetable oil. When the oil is hot, pour a thin layer of the crêpe mixture into the centre of the pan. Tilt the pan until the mixture spreads over the entire surface. Cook the batter briefly until golden brown. Flip the crêpe and lightly brown the reverse side. Slide the crêpe onto a plate and keep warm.

Leftover batter can be refrigerated for up to 4 days.

To make the wild mushroom filling, rehydrate the mushrooms according to the instructions on the packet. Heat the oil in a pan and fry the onions and garlic over a low heat until translucent. Add the mushrooms and herbs and sauté until soft. Season to taste. Add the cream and reduce the mixture for about 7 minutes over a high heat.

Spoon the mixture onto one half of the crêpe. Fold the other half of the crepé over the filling.

Garnish with truffle oil and Parmesan cheese.

Suggested wine: Sauvignon Blanc

Lentil Salad with Lettuce

Serves 6

250 ml brown lentils
2 onions, thinly sliced
1 dried bay leaf
salt
45 ml extra virgin olive oil
1 medium aubergine, chopped
250 g button mushrooms, chopped
1 red pepper, chopped
1 green pepper, chopped
1 yellow pepper, chopped
1 clove garlic, crushed
3 tomatoes, diced
15 ml tomato paste
15 ml balsamic vinegar
Lettuce leaves for garnish
6 boiled quail eggs for garnish

Soak the lentils overnight in water and strain the next morning.

Boil the lentils, the slices of 1 onion and the bay leaf for about 10 minutes in a pot with salted water. Strain the mixture through a sieve.

Heat the oil and fry the remaining onion slices, aubergine, mushrooms, peppers, garlic and tomatoes. Add the tomato paste. Sauté for 10 minutes over a moderate heat. Add the lentils and sauté for a further 5 minutes. Remove the mixture from the heat. Stir in the balsamic vinegar.

Serve garnished with lettuce and boiled quail eggs.

Suggested wine: Sauvignon Blanc

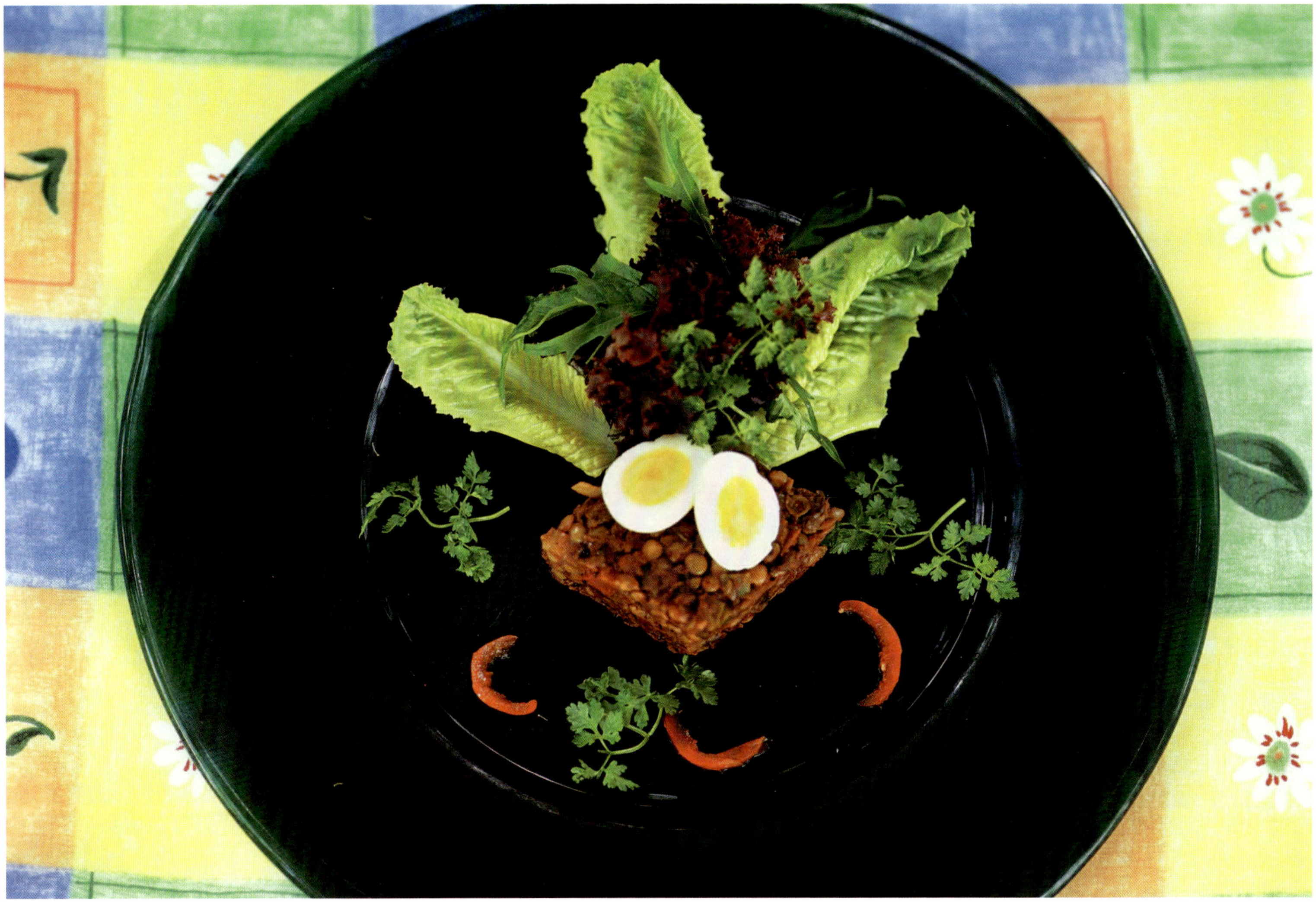

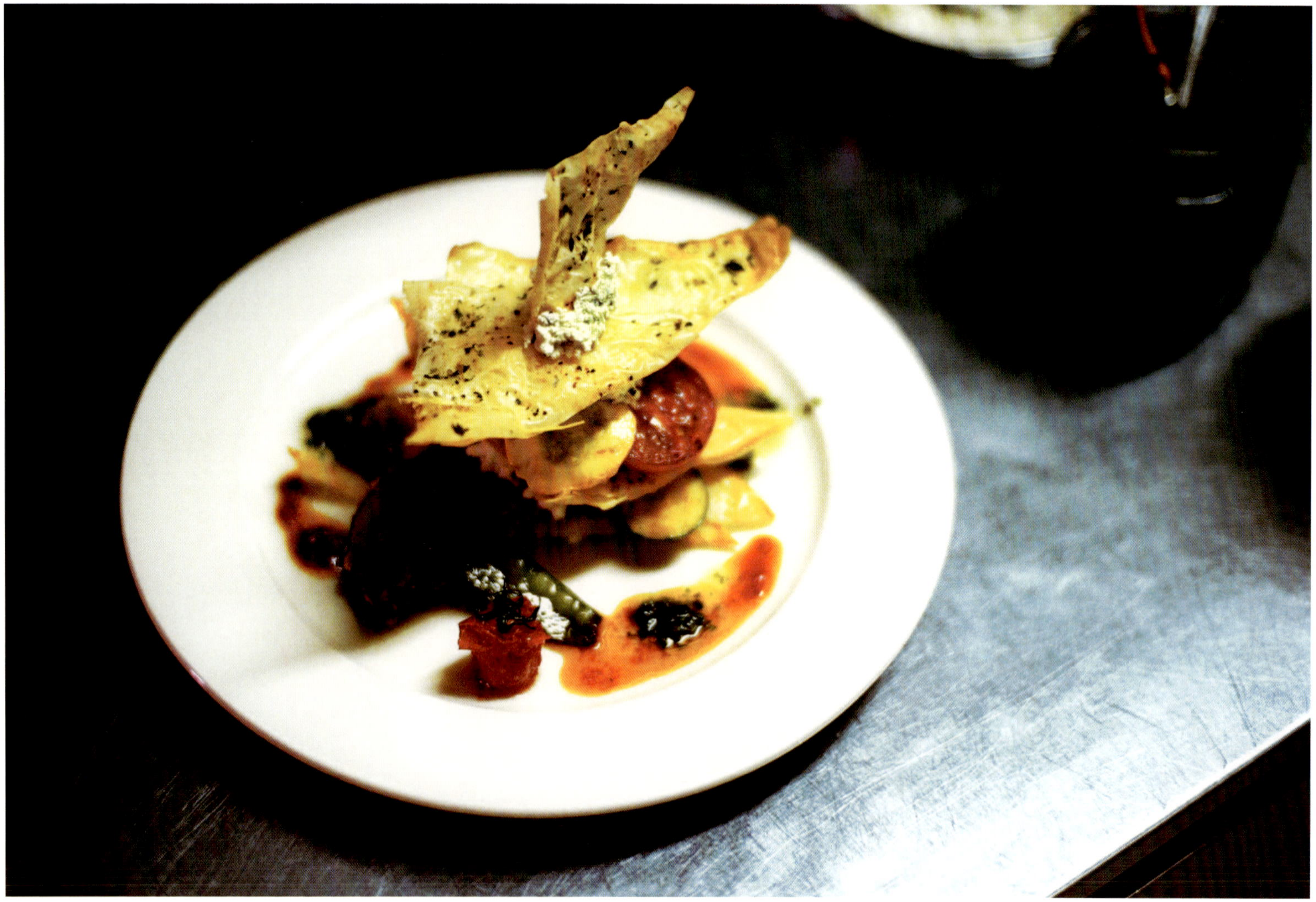

Vegetable Mille Feuille with Basil Pesto and Red Pepper Coulis

Serves 4

2 red peppers
2 yellow peppers
3 courgettes, sliced diagonally
4 yellow patty pan squashes, sliced diagonally
100 ml melted herb butter
2 medium aubergines
2 eggs, whisked
40 ml grated Parmesan cheese
vegetable oil for frying
12 phyllo pastry sheets
aubergine caviar (page 33)
200 g ricotta cheese

Basil pesto

250 ml basil, chopped
250 ml extra virgin olive oil
1 clove garlic, whole
15 ml pine kernels
50 ml grated Parmesan cheese
salt & pepper to taste

Red pepper coulis

2 red peppers, seeded
125 ml red wine vinegar
45 g sugar
salt & pepper

Preheat the oven grill.

Halve the peppers and remove the seeds and stems. Brush the peppers, courgettes and patty pans with 60 ml of the melted herb butter. Chargrill the vegetables for 2 minutes on each side.

Cut the aubergines into 1 cm thick slices. Dip the slices into a bowl of whisked egg and then into the Parmesan. Deep-fry in oil until golden brown. Drain the aubergine slices on towelling paper.

Cut the phyllo pastry sheets into shapes of your choice. Brush the pastry with the remaining melted herb butter and layer 2 sheets on top of one another. Bake at 180 °C until golden brown.

When ready to serve, arrange alternate layers of the vegetables, aubergine caviar and ricotta cheese and the phyllo pastry shapes. If desired, serve while the vegetables are still hot.

Drizzle with basil pesto and red pepper coulis.

To make the basil pesto, place all the ingredients, except the oil, in a food processor. Blend for about 30 seconds and then add the oil by pouring it slowly through the top of the food processor. If you do this too quickly, the pesto will separate. If it does separate, simply add 10 ml of cold water while processing. Keep refrigerated.

Make the red pepper coulis by blending the peppers in a food processor. Place in a saucepan and add the vinegar and sugar. Reduce the mixture for 10 minutes over a moderate heat until a thick consistency is achieved. Strain through a sieve and season to taste.

Suggested wine: Sauvignon Blanc

Serves 4

Mayonnaise

1 egg yolk
2.5 ml white malt vinegar
2.5 ml English mustard
salt & pepper to taste
250 ml extra virgin olive oil

Tartare

200 g ostrich fillet
1 onion, finely chopped
5 capers, finely chopped
3 gherkins, finely chopped
100 ml fresh parsley, chopped
salt & pepper to taste
4 raw quail eggs
homemade brown bread

Ostrich Tartare

To make the mayonnaise place the egg yolk, vinegar, mustard and seasoning in a food processor and blend until smooth. Slowly add the oil until the desired thickness is achieved. Season to taste. Refrigerate the mayonnaise.

Chop the ostrich fillet finely. In a bowl, mix the fillet, onion, capers, gherkins, parsley and mayonnaise. Season to taste.

Form the mixture into two or three small ovals on each plate. Top with raw quail eggs and serve with slices of homemade brown bread.

Suggested wine: Sauvignon Blanc

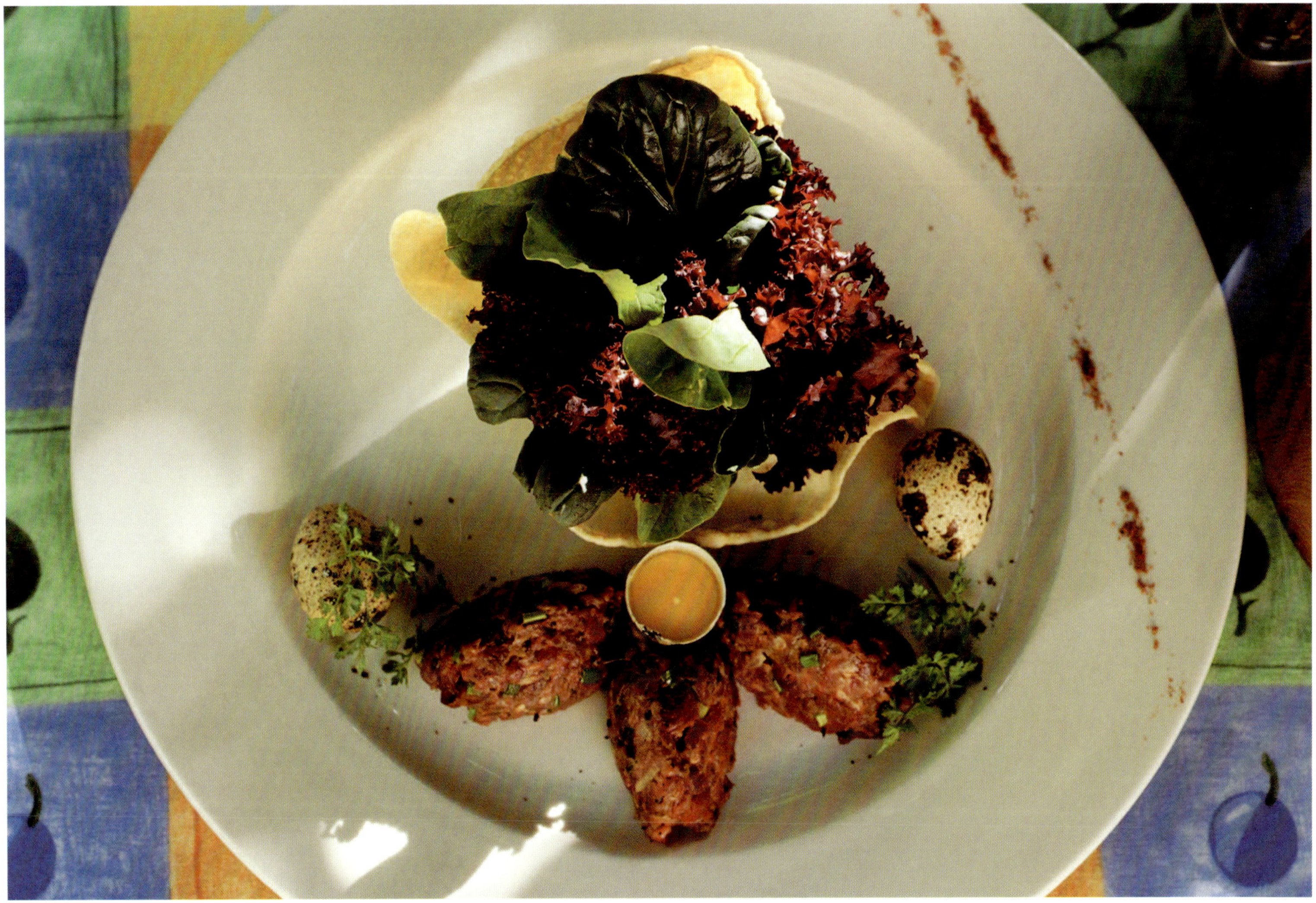

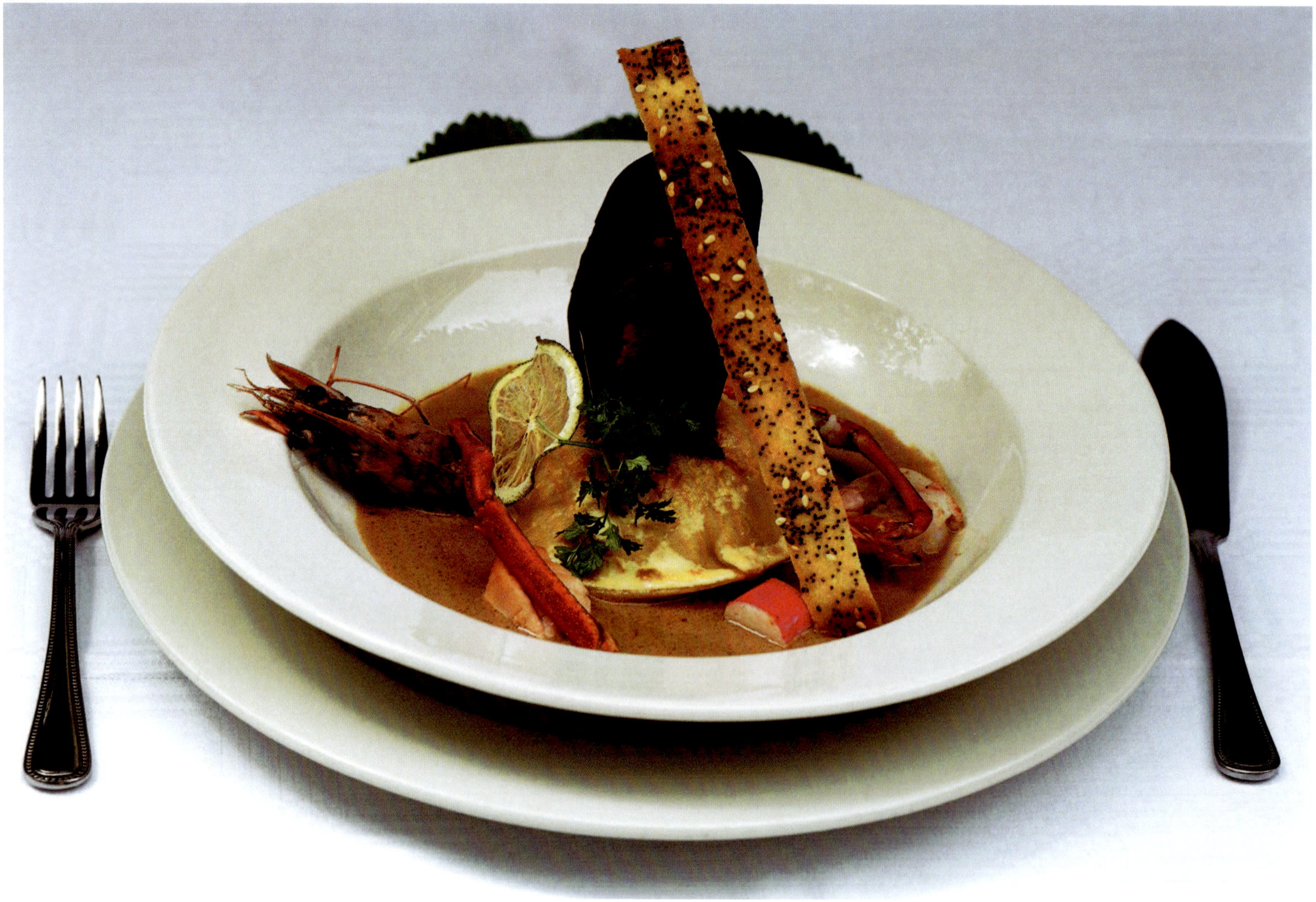

Serves 6

350 g cake flour
4 egg yolks
2 eggs
125 ml extra virgin olive oil
salt
bisque sauce (page 60)
fresh fennel for garnish

Fish filling

200 g filleted fish of your choice, skin removed
1 egg white
45 ml fresh fennel, chopped
45 ml fresh coriander, chopped
250 ml cream
salt & pepper
6 mussels
6 prawns
grated Parmesan cheese

Seafood Ravioli

Place the cake flour, egg yolks, eggs, oil and salt in a food processor and blend until smooth. Leave to rest for 30 minutes. Using a pasta machine, roll the dough to the desired thickness (about 1 mm). We recommend you set your machine to no. 5.

To make the filling, place the fish, egg white, fennel, coriander and cream in a food processor and blend until smooth. Season to taste.

Spoon 6 mounds (30 ml each) of the filling onto the pasta. Working lengthways, place the filling just below the centre of the pasta strip. Leave at least 7.5 cm between each mound. Put 1 mussel and 1 prawn on top of each mound of filling. Brush the strip of dough with egg white to help the ravioli hold together. Fold the top half of the pasta over the filling. Press between each ravioli and around the sides to seal the filling. Use a ravioli cutter to separate the ravioli.

Simmer the ravioli squares in a pot of salted water for 7 minutes. Remove the ravioli from the water with a sieve and drain. Top with grated Parmesan and grill until golden brown.

To serve, pour bisque sauce over the top and garnish with fresh fennel.

Suggested wine: Chardonnay or Semillon

Willowbrook Thai Fishcakes

Serves 6

300 g filleted fish of your choice, skin removed
50 ml chopped fennel
200 g mashed potatoes
juice of 1 lemon
salt & pepper
100 g cake flour
2 eggs, lightly beaten
100 g white breadcrumbs
vegetable oil for frying
fresh coriander for garnish
1 bottle sweet Thai chilli sauce (available in most supermarkets)

Preheat the oven to 180 °C.

Lightly fry the fish with half of the fennel until soft. Remove from the heat and leave to cool. Flake the fish with a fork. Then mix the mashed potato, remaining fennel and lemon juice with the fish. Season to taste. Roll the mixture into 6 fishcakes. Dip them in the flour and then the egg. Coat with the breadcrumbs. Deep-fry in vegetable oil until golden brown.

Place the fishcakes in the oven for 10 minutes.

Garnish with fresh coriander and serve with sweet Thai chilli sauce and a salad of your choice.

Suggested wine: Chenin Blanc

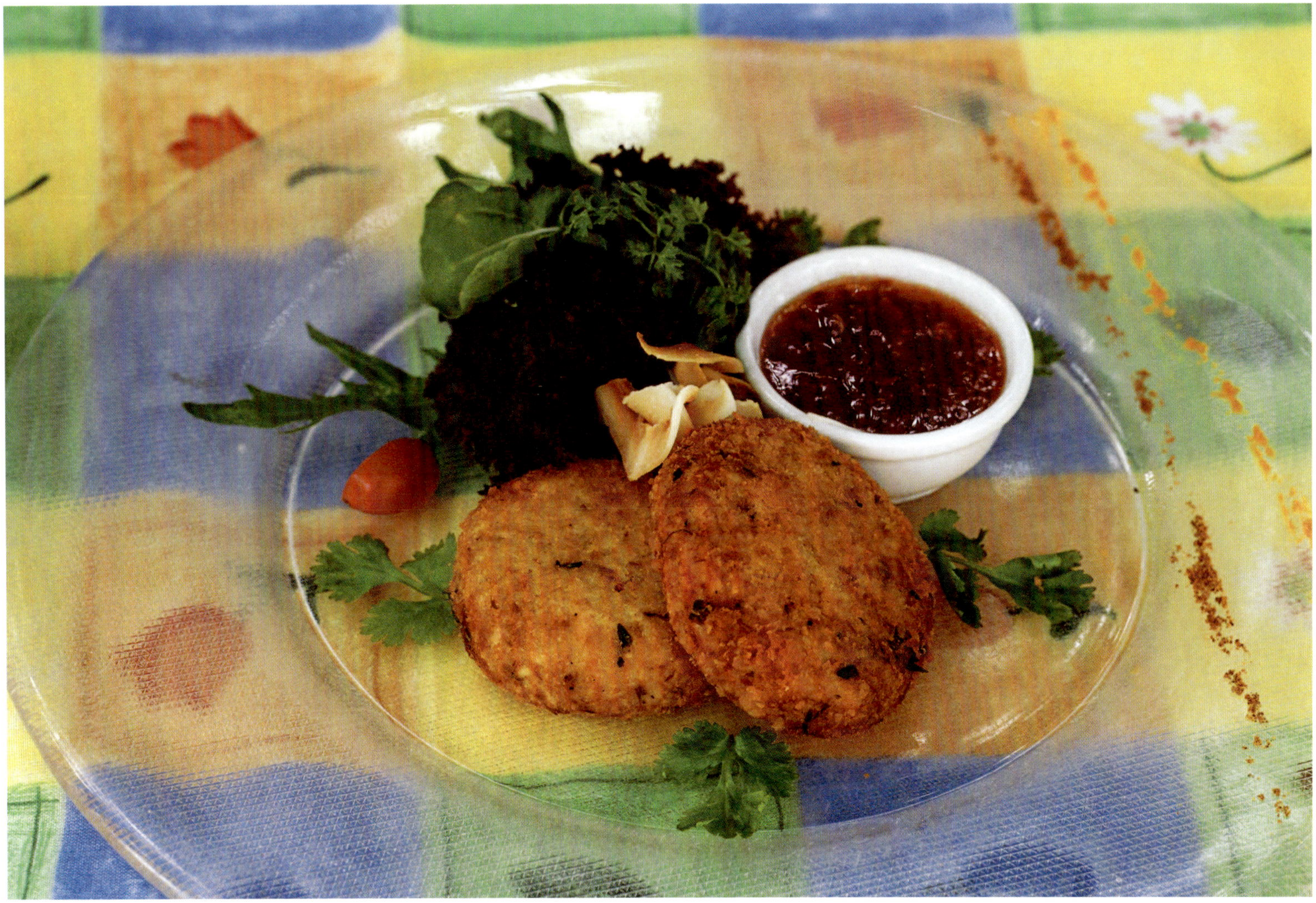

A smiling face is half the meal.

LATVIAN PROVERB

Mains

Loran chooses Cape salmon at the nearby Gordon's Bay jetty. Only the freshest linefish will do.

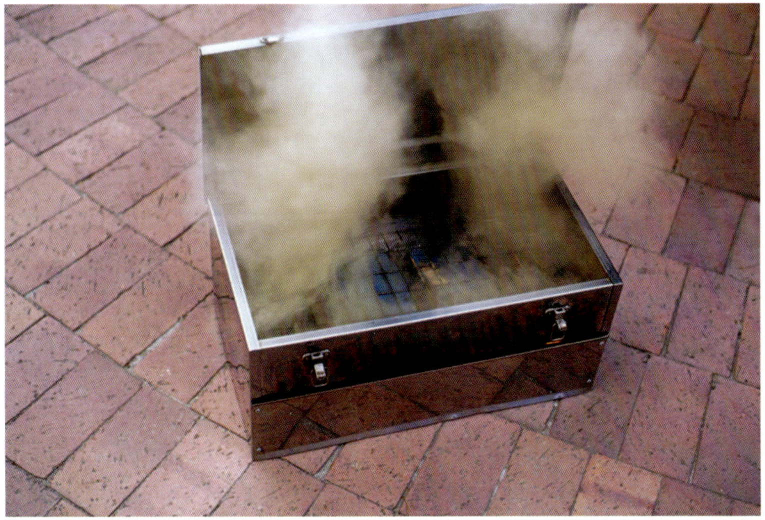
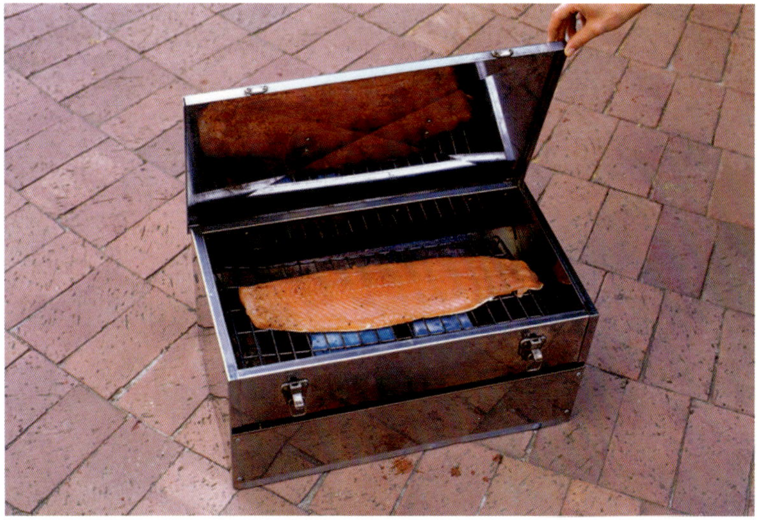
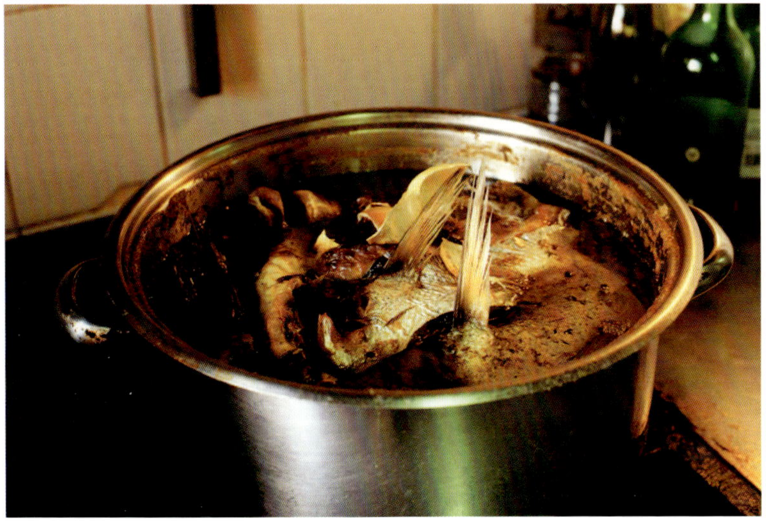
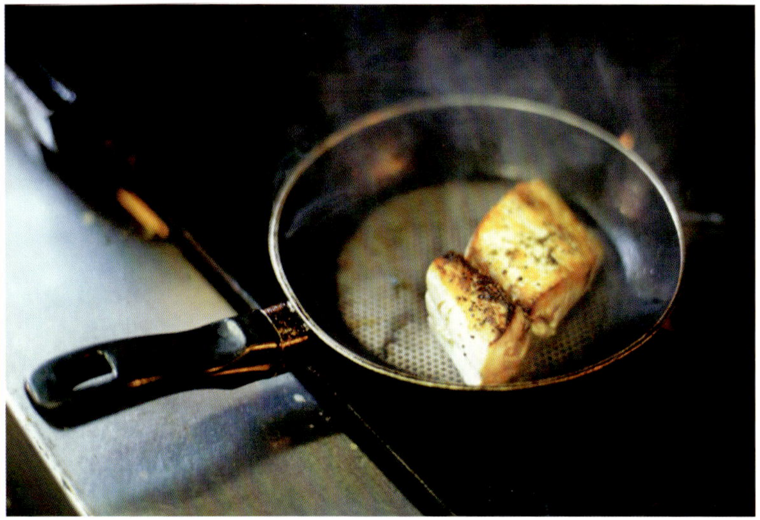

Serves 4

4 large potatoes, peeled
salt & pepper to taste
2 eggs
20 ml chives, chopped
vegetable oil for frying

Toppings

120 g Camembert cheese
4 cherry tomatoes
100 g smoked salmon
15 g salted butter
200 g button mushrooms, sliced
15 ml fresh thyme
200 ml cream

Trio of Rösti

Preheat the oven to 180 °C.

Grate the potatoes and squeeze out the excess water. Add the seasoning, eggs and chives to the grated potato. Press the mixture into flattened pancake shapes, 5 cm round and 1 cm thick. Pan-fry the rösti on both sides in hot oil until brown. Bake for 10 minutes. Serve three portions per plate, topped with:

- grilled Camembert cheese and cherry tomatoes

- smoked salmon

- mushroom sauce.

To prepare the mushroom sauce, sauté the mushrooms in the butter. Add the thyme and cream, then reduce the sauce over a moderate heat until the mixture becomes thick.

Garnish with a small salad of your choice.

Suggested wine: Semillon

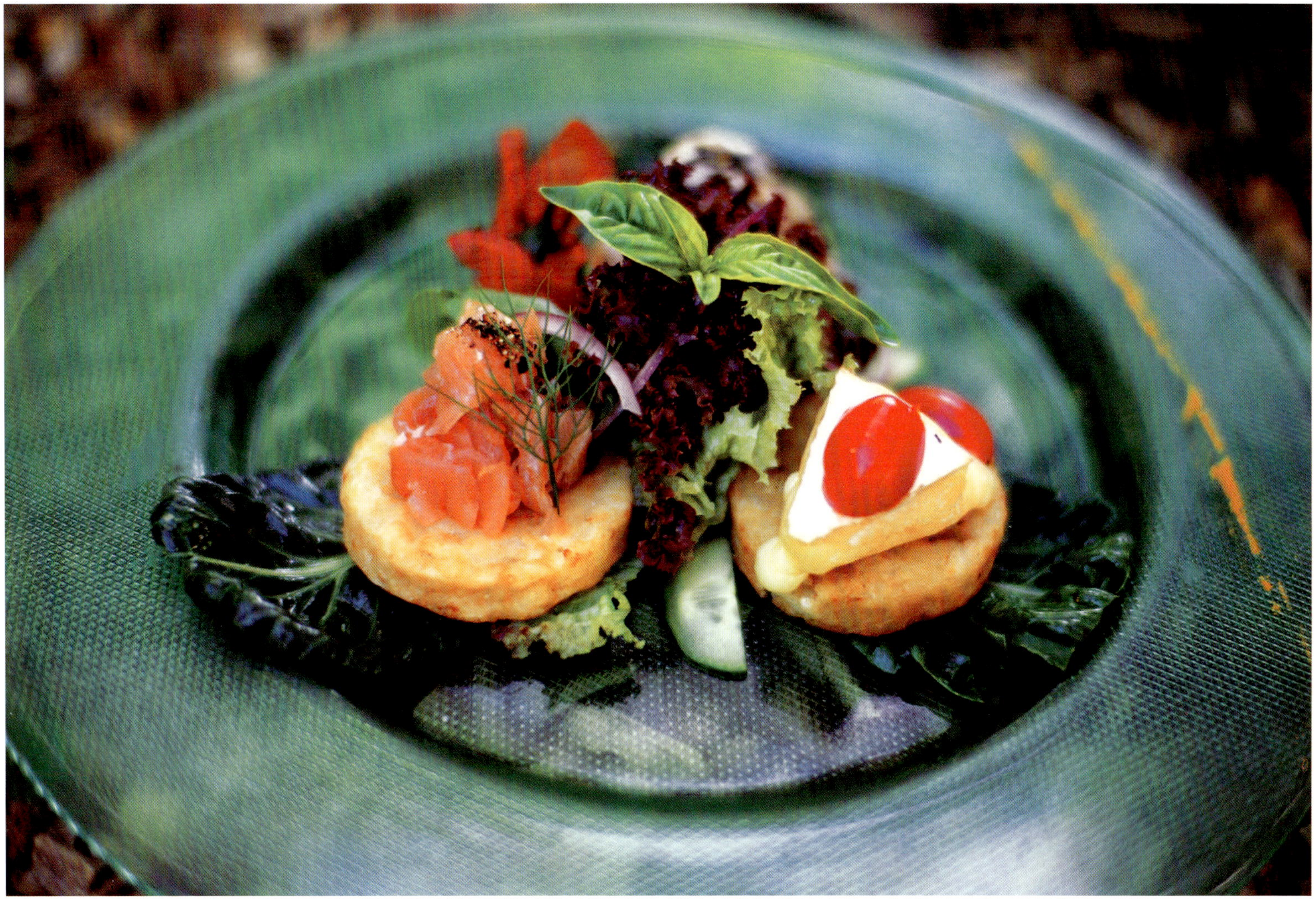

Chickpea chips 500 ml water
30 ml extra virgin olive oil
175 g chickpea flour
salt & pepper
vegetable oil for frying

Saffron sauce 2 g saffron
100 ml white wine
200 ml cream
salt & pepper

Linefish Chermoula with Tempura Oysters, Chickpea Chips and Saffron Sauce

Serves 4

4 x 150 g pieces of firm white fish (for example, kingklip, Cape salmon, cob)
2 small red chillies, seeded and chopped
50 ml coriander, chopped
50 ml fennel or dill, chopped
25 ml extra virgin olive oil
salt & pepper

Tomato and cumin crust

200 g sun-dried tomatoes
25 g ground cumin
200 g white breadcrumbs
150 ml melted butter
salt & pepper

Tempura oysters

85 g cake flour
85 g corn flour
15 g baking powder
150 ml water
15 ml extra virgin olive oil
4 oysters
vegetable oil for frying

Preheat the oven to 180 °C.

Coat the fish with the chilli, coriander, fennel (or dill) and oil. Marinate the fish in the fridge for 30 minutes until ready to use.

Blend all the ingredients for the tomato and cumin crust in a food processor. Roll the mixture thinly onto greaseproof paper. Refrigerate until needed.

Prepare the batter for the tempura oysters by mixing the cake flour, corn flour, baking powder, water and olive oil in a bowl. Dip the oysters into the batter and deep-fry in hot vegetable oil until golden.

To make the saffron sauce, combine the saffron, wine, cream, salt and pepper in a saucepan and reduce until the sauce has reached pouring consistency.

In the meantime, boil the water and oil in a pot to make the chickpea chips. Mix in the chickpea flour and stir over a low heat for approximately 5 minutes. Remove the chickpea mixture from the heat and roll it out onto a baking tray. The base should be about 1 cm thick. Put it in the fridge to set. When cold, cut the dough into rectangular strips, about 4 cm long and 1 cm wide. Deep-fry the chips in hot vegetable oil until golden brown.

When ready to serve, remove the marinated fish from the fridge and transfer to an ovenproof dish. Cover each piece of fish with the tomato and cumin crust mixture. Bake for 10 minutes. Serve the fish topped with a tempura oyster and pour over the saffron sauce. Arrange the chickpea chips on the plate.

Suggested wine: Pinot Noir

Fish Petit Farcis

Serves 4

4 x 150 g fish fillets (for example, kingklip, cob, red roman)
10 ml extra virgin olive oil
4 medium patty pan squashes
4 medium tomatoes
2 courgettes, cut in half
salt & pepper to taste
red pepper coulis (page 41)
fresh dill for garnish

Ratatouille

10 ml extra virgin olive oil
1 onion, finely chopped
1 garlic clove, crushed
½ red pepper, chopped
1 small aubergine, chopped
2 courgettes, chopped
5 ml tomato paste
5 ml fresh thyme, chopped
salt & pepper to taste

Polenta

250 ml polenta
15 ml fresh herbs (chopped thyme and basil)
350 ml full cream milk
salt & pepper

Preheat the oven to 180 °C.

Heat the oil and pan-fry the fish for 5 minutes on each side. Set aside.

Prepare the ratatouille by pan-frying the onion and garlic in the oil until soft. Add the red pepper, aubergine, courgettes, tomato paste and thyme and simmer for 5 minutes.

Hollow out the yellow patty pans and blanch for 5 minutes. Remove the patty pans from the water, drain and fill with ratatouille.

Sauté the mushrooms with the herbs, salt and pepper in the oil and set aside. Hollow out the courgettes and blanch for 5 minutes. Remove the courgettes from the water, drain and fill with sautéed mushrooms.

Mix the polenta, 15 ml fresh herbs and milk in a saucepan. Cook slowly over a moderate heat until thickened. Season to taste. Hollow out the tomatoes and fill with polenta.

Put the fish fillets and vegetables on a greased baking tray and heat in the oven for 10 minutes.

Assemble the dish by placing the fish in the centre of the plate and arranging the petit farcis around it.

Drizzle with red pepper coulis and garnish with fresh dill.

Mushrooms

250 g button mushrooms, sliced
10 ml extra virgin olive oil
15 ml fresh herbs (chopped thyme and basil)
salt & pepper

Suggested wine: Sauvignon Blanc

Fish stock 500 g fish bones
1 litre water
1 whole onion, halved
1 leek, washed and roughly chopped

3 carrots, roughly chopped
3 celery sticks, roughly chopped
1 bouquet garni (1 bay leaf and 2 sprigs each of fennel, thyme and parsley)
5 black pepper corns

Serves 4

4 x 180 g Norwegian salmon
50 ml poppy seeds
25 ml sesame seeds (white and black)
5 ml aniseed
20 ml extra virgin olive oil for frying
salt & pepper to taste
250 ml fish stock
50 ml white wine
250 ml cream
20 pitted black olives
salt & pepper

Sauce

250 ml fish stock (page 58)
50 ml white wine
250 ml cream
20 pitted black olives
salt & pepper

Poached fennel bulbs

2 fennel bulbs, cut in half
100 ml white wine
200 ml water
2 garlic cloves, whole
salt & pepper to taste
chervil for garnish

Chive mashed potato

4 large potatoes
40 ml fresh chives, chopped
salt & pepper

Seed-crusted Norwegian Salmon with Poached Fennel Bulbs and Chive Mashed Potato

Prepare the fish stock in advance. Combine all the ingredients for the stock in a large pot and simmer over a low heat for approximately 1.5 hours. Strain the stock and refrigerate until needed. Leftover stock can be frozen.

Preheat the oven to 180 °C.

Mix the poppy seeds, sesame seeds and aniseed in a shallow bowl. Heat the oil and pan-fry the salmon for 2 minutes on each side. Then roll the fish in the seeds. Just before serving, place the salmon in the oven for 5 minutes.

Make the sauce by combining the fish stock, wine and cream in a saucepan. Simmer the mixture over a low heat until the sauce thickens. Add the olives and season well.

To make the poached fennel bulbs, place the fennel bulbs, cut side down, in an ovenproof dish. Add the wine, water and garlic. Season to taste. Cover the dish with tin foil and place in the oven for 35 minutes at 160 °C or until the bulbs are soft.

In a pot, bring salted water to the boil. Add the potatoes and cook until soft. Mash the potatoes and mix in the chives. Season to taste.

Assemble the dish by placing the fish on a bed of mashed potato in the centre of the plate. Place one piece of fennel bulb next to the fish and dress with the sauce.

Garnish with chervil.

Suggested wine: Pinot Noir

Serves 4

28 black tiger prawns
30 ml extra virgin olive oil
10 ml Cajun spice
salt & pepper to taste
100 ml couscous
100 ml water
100 ml coriander, chopped
4 medium tomatoes
4 baby carrots
4 baby corn
4 French green beans
coriander pesto*

Bisque sauce

500 g prawn and crayfish shells
15 ml extra virgin olive oil
5 ml tomato paste
100 ml fennel
50 ml port
50 ml brandy
2 carrots, chopped
1 onion, chopped
1 celery stalk, chopped
1 litre water
250 ml cream
salt & pepper to taste

Tiger Prawns with Couscous and Bisque Sauce

Remove the shells of the prawns but not the heads and tails. Heat the oil in a frying pan over a moderate to high heat. Fry the prawns for approximately 2 minutes on each side until their colour changes. Season with the spice, salt and pepper when turning the prawns over. Make sure you do not overcook the prawns.

Place the couscous and water in a saucepan and gently bring to the boil over a moderate heat. Cook until the water has evaporated. Remove the couscous from the heat and add the coriander. Add salt and pepper to taste.

Cut the tops off the tomatoes. Hollow out the tomatoes and blanch them for 5 minutes. Blanch the carrots, corn and green beans for 5 minutes and strain. Fill the tomatoes with one of each of the blanched vegetables. You could substitute cauliflower or broccoli florets for the baby corn and green beans.

To make the bisque sauce, heat the oil in a large saucepan. Brown the prawn and crayfish shells in the oil over a high heat. Add the tomato paste and cook for 5 minutes. Add the port. Flambé the sauce by adding the brandy, heating it through, and igniting it. When flames are extinguished, add the vegetables, cover with water and simmer for 1 hour over a low heat. Mix in the cream and reduce the sauce over a moderate heat until a pouring consistency is reached. Strain through a sieve.

To assemble the dish, place the couscous in the centre of the plate and arrange 7 prawns per portion around it. Place the filled tomato next to the couscous. Pour 25 ml of the bisque sauce over the prawns and drizzle with 5 ml coriander pesto.

Garnish with fresh coriander.

* Follow the recipe for basil pesto on page 41 but substitute the coriander for the basil.

Suggested wine: Chardonnay

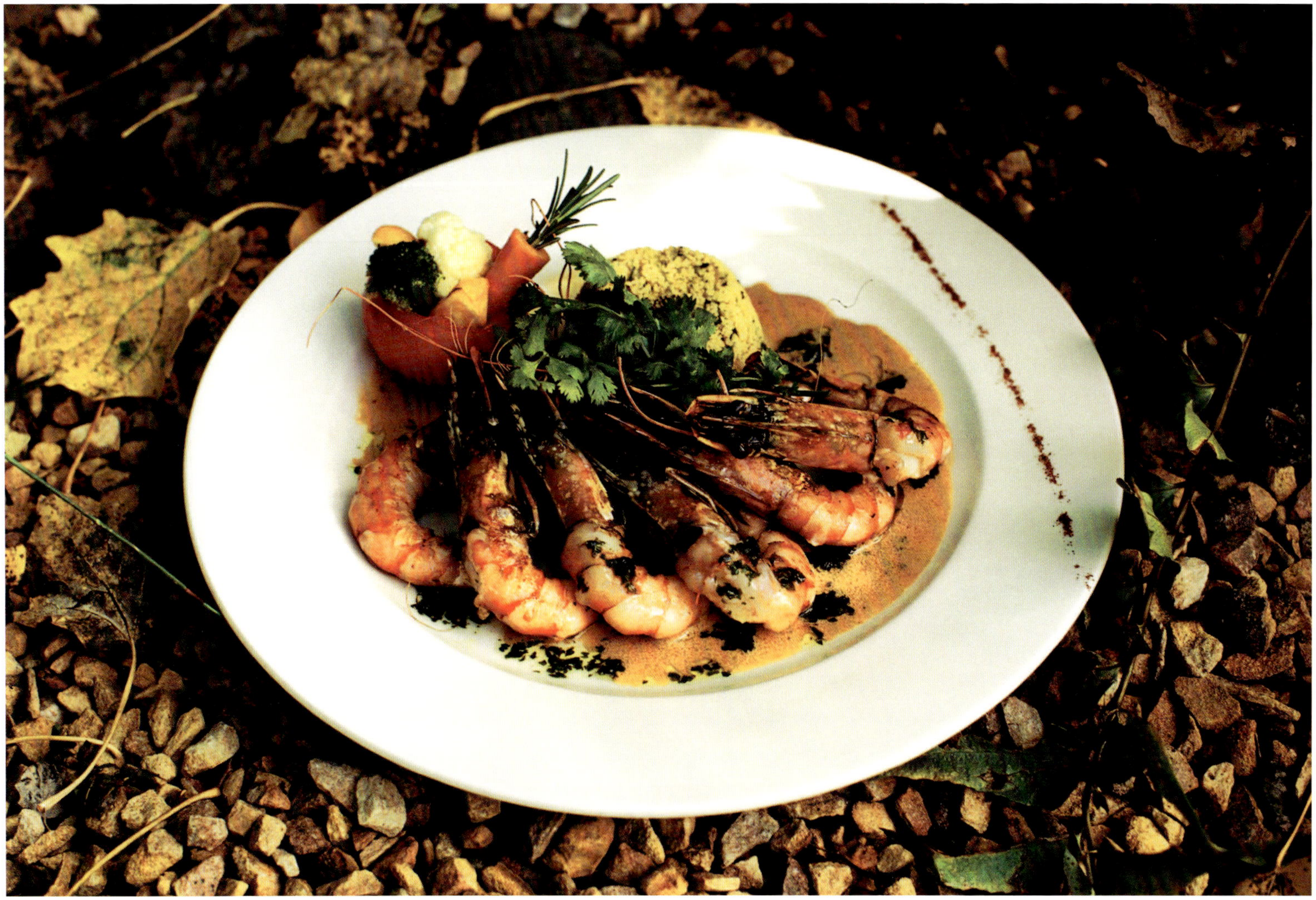

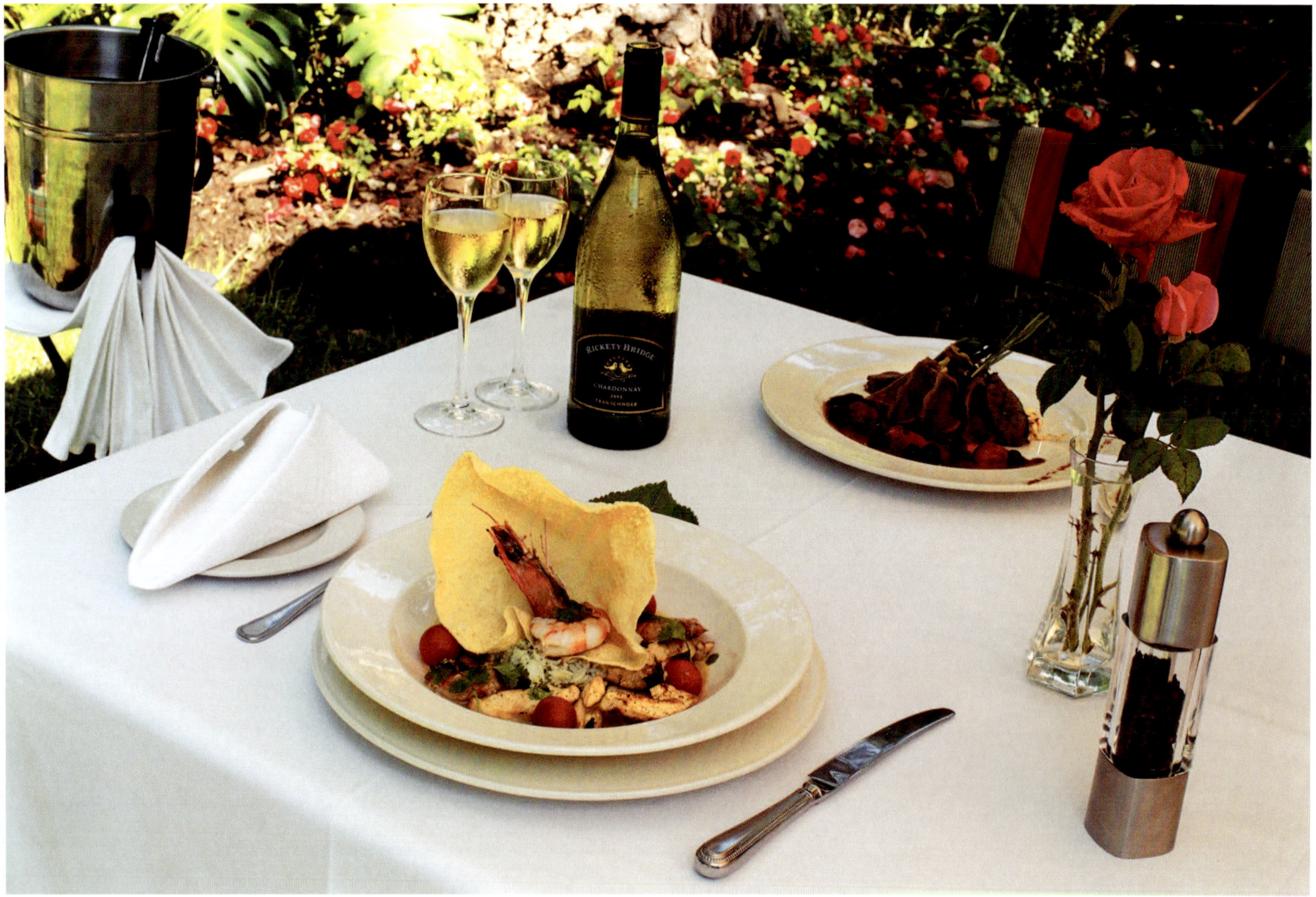
RICKETY BRIDGE
CHARDONNAY

Thai Green Chicken and Prawn Curry

Serves 4

12 prawns
500 g chicken breasts, cut into strips
20 ml extra virgin olive oil
450 ml coconut milk
40 ml coriander, chopped
5 ml green Thai curry paste
250 ml basmati rice, raw
600 ml water
salt & pepper to taste
4 popadams for garnish
12 cherry tomatoes for garnish
fresh coriander for garnish

Remove the shells of the prawns but not the heads and tails. Pan-fry the chicken in the oil for approximately 4 minutes over a high heat. Add the coconut milk, coriander, curry paste and prawns and reduce the sauce over a relatively high heat for 5–7 minutes.

Place the basmati rice in a heat-resistant colander. In a saucepan, bring 600 ml water to the boil. Reduce the heat and simmer. Place the colander inside the saucepan and close the lid. Steam the rice for 20–25 minutes until soft and season well. When opening and closing the lid, take care not to burn yourself with the steam.

Prepare the popadams according to the instructions on the packet.

To assemble the dish, spoon the rice in the centre of the plate and surround it with the curry.

Garnish with popadams, cherry tomatoes and fresh coriander.

Suggested wine: Chenin Blanc

Serves 4

4 x 180 g springbok fillets
20 ml coarse black pepper
15 ml extra virgin olive oil
500 g green beans, blanched
rosemary stalks for garnish

Spatzle

250 g cake flour, sifted
190 ml full cream milk
1 egg yolk
2 ml ground nutmeg
salt & pepper to taste
10 ml extra virgin olive oil
1.5 litres water
15 ml salt

Hot minted strawberries

50 g sugar
100 ml raspberry vinegar
20 g refrigerated butter, cut into 1 cm blocks
10 strawberries, topped and halved
15 ml fresh mint, chopped

Black Pepper-crusted Springbok with Hot Minted Strawberries and Spatzle

Roll the springbok fillets in the black pepper. Heat the oil in a saucepan and fry the fillets for 2 minutes on each side to seal in the meat juices. The meat is now cooked medium-rare. Do not overcook the springbok as it could become tough.

Remove the fillets from the heat and slice the springbok into 1-cm slices at an angle.

Combine all the ingredients for the spatzle, except the water and salt, in a mixing bowl. Cover the dough with a damp cloth and leave to rest for 15 minutes.

In a large saucepan, bring to the boil 1.5 litres of water with 15 ml salt. Using a colander with big holes, put 3 large spoons of the spatzle mixture into the colander at a time and force it through the holes into the boiling water. When the dough boils to the top of the surface, the spatzle is cooked through.

Transfer the spatzle to a bowl of cold water filled with ice. Strain and refrigerate until needed. The refrigerated spatzle will keep up to 3 days.

When ready to serve, heat the oil in a saucepan over a high heat. Add the spatzle, season and fry until brown and crispy. Drain on towelling paper.

To make the minted strawberries, caramelise the sugar in a saucepan over a moderate heat until light brown in colour. Add the raspberry vinegar and reduce for 5 minutes. Remove from the heat and whisk in the butter blocks, one at a time, until melted. Add the strawberries and mint. Serve while still hot.

To assemble the dish, place the spatzle in the centre of the plate and arrange the springbok slices at an angle against the spatzle. Drizzle the hot minted strawberries over the meat, allowing about 5 strawberry halves per person.

Serve with blanched green beans and garnish with rosemary stalks.

Suggested wine: Shiraz or Rubicon

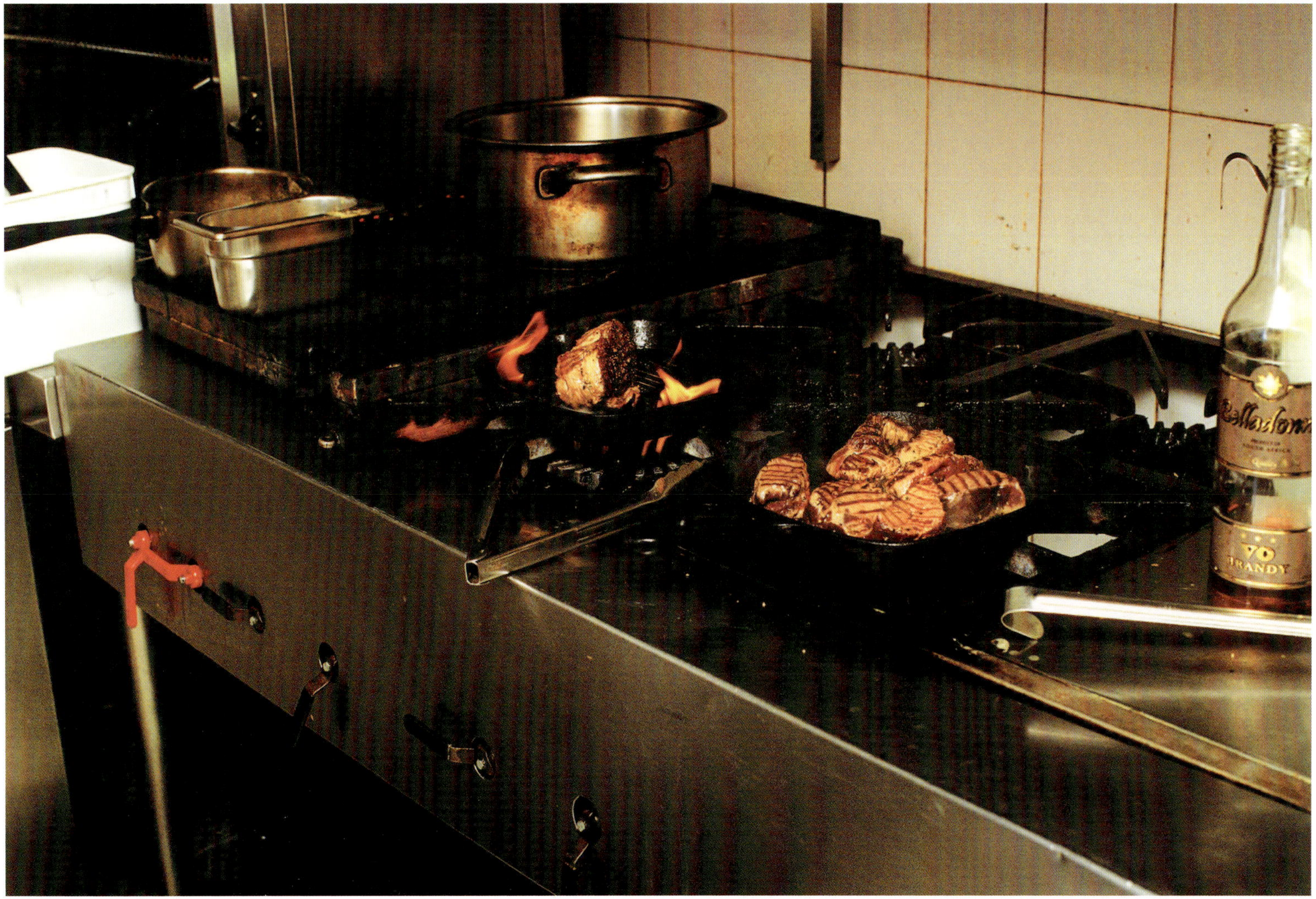
VO
BRANDY

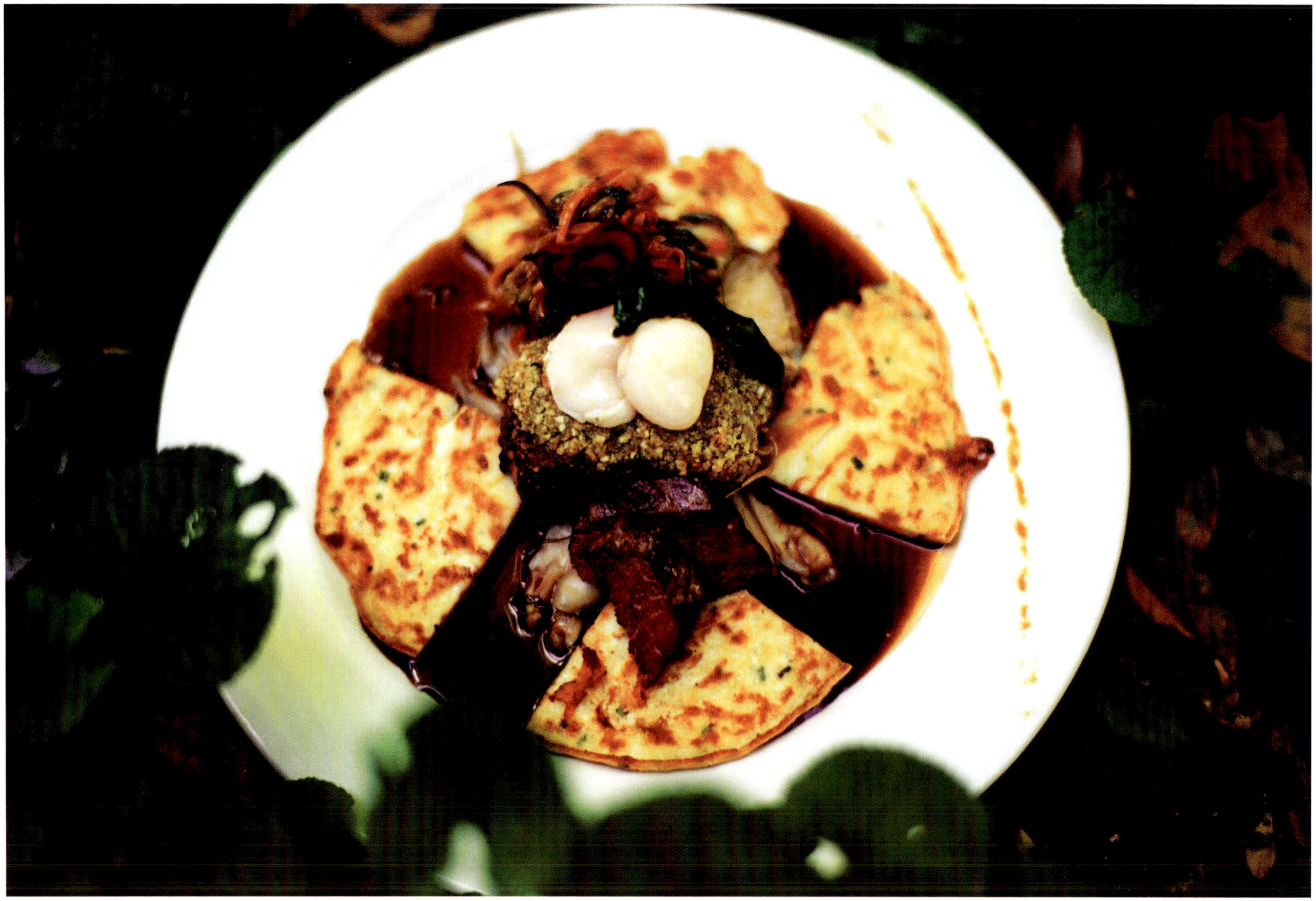

Pistachio-crusted Ostrich Medallions with Potato Galettes

Serves 4

4 x 150 g ostrich fillet medallions
salt & pepper to taste
15 ml extra virgin olive oil
rosemary and honey sauce (page 71)
fresh litchis for garnish

Pistachio crust

100 ml pistachio nuts, shelled
40 ml chopped herbs (thyme, parsley and basil)
50 ml breadcrumbs
1 clove garlic
70 ml melted butter
salt & pepper to taste

Potato galettes

375 g mashed potato
60 g flour
75 g smooth cottage cheese
4 eggs
75 ml chopped chives
salt & pepper
15 ml extra virgin olive oil

Preheat the oven to 180 °C.

Season the meat. Heat the oil in a saucepan over a moderate heat and fry the medallions for 2 minutes on each side to seal in the meat juices. Remove the ostrich medallions from the heat.

Blend the pistachio nuts, herbs, breadcrumbs, garlic, melted butter, salt and pepper in a food processor until coarse. Top each of the medallions with the pistachio crust and bake for 7 minutes.

Mix all the ingredients for the potato galettes in a mixing bowl. Heat the oil in a crêpe pan or other small pan (approximately 20 cm in diameter). Scoop a quarter of the potato mixture into the pan and press to form a round cake about 1 cm thick. Cook for 5 minutes over a low heat until brown, then turn over and cook for 5 more minutes. Remove the galette from the pan and cut into quarters. Repeat until you have made 4 galettes.

Dish one ostrich medallion per person. Place the medallions on top of the galettes and serve with rosemary and honey sauce.

Garnish with fresh litchis.

Suggested wine: Merlot

Veal Medallions with Tagliatelle, Onions and Marsala Sauce

Serves 4

8 x 75 g veal medallions
salt & pepper
8 sage leaves
8 thin slices of Parma ham
15 ml extra virgin olive oil
300 g tagliatelle, cooked
150 ml cream
15 ml chives, chopped
zest and juice of 1 lemon
fresh sage leaves for garnish

Onions

8 baby onions or shallots
250 ml red wine
250 ml balsamic vinegar
1 bay leaf
salt & pepper to taste

Marsala sauce

15 ml Marsala or full cream sherry
250 ml cream
250 ml veal or chicken stock
salt & pepper to taste

Preheat the oven to 180 °C.

Season the veal and wrap each medallion with one sage leaf and one slice of Parma ham. Heat the oil in a frying pan over a moderate heat. Place the veal in the pan and brown for approximately 5 minutes, turning the meat while cooking. Just before serving, place the medallions in the oven for 5 minutes.

Combine the tagliatelle, cream, chives and lemon zest and juice in a pot and heat through over a low heat.

Peel the onions and place in an ovenproof dish. Add the red wine, balsamic vinegar and bay leaf and cook in the oven at 200 °C for 20 minutes or until soft. Season to taste.

In a saucepan, mix together all the ingredients for the Marsala sauce. Reduce over a moderate heat until a pouring consistency is reached.

To assemble, put the tagliatelle in the centre of the plate and place the medallions on top. Serve 2 baby onions per plate. Drizzle the sauce over the veal.

Garnish with fresh sage leaves.

Suggested wine: Merlot

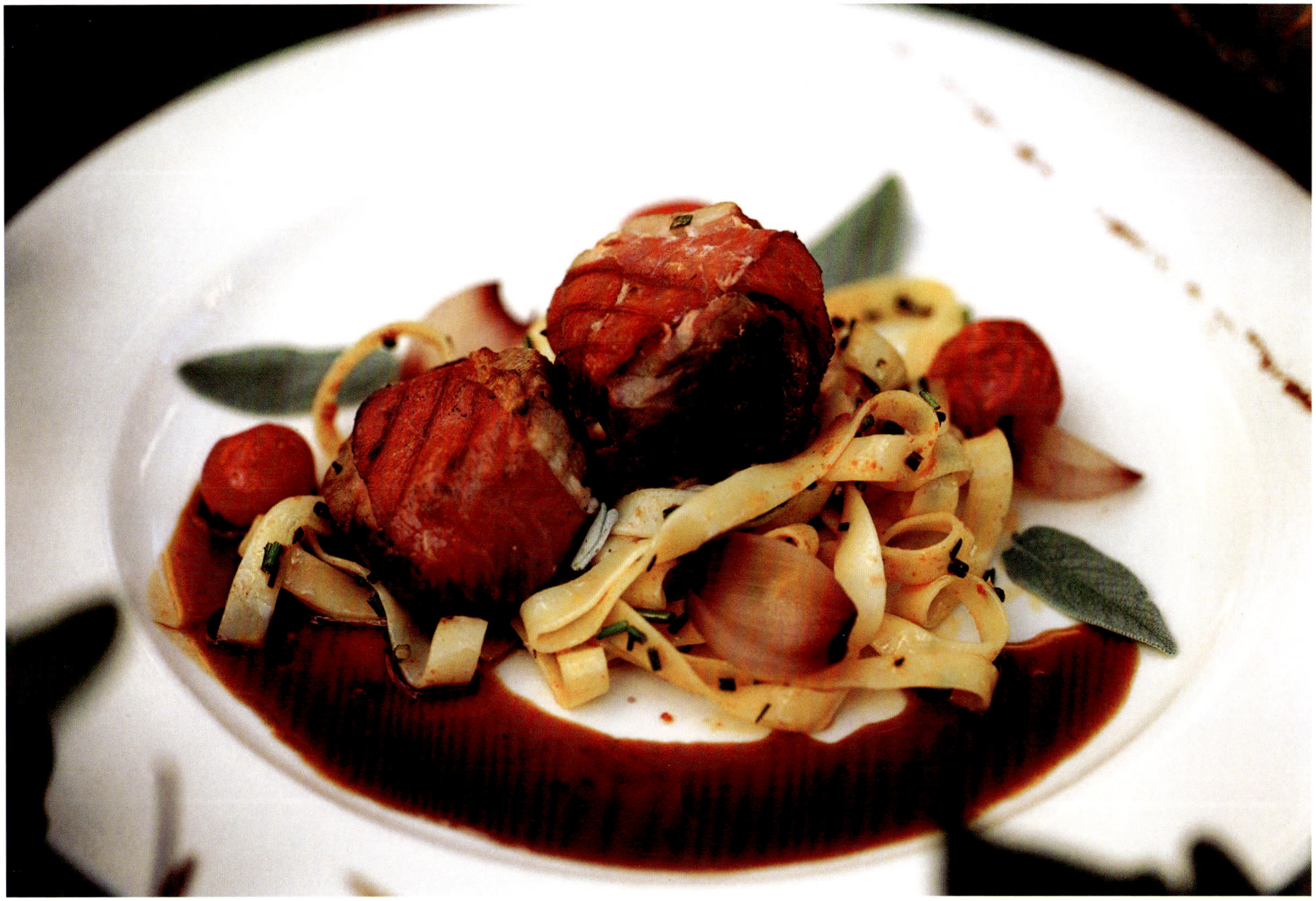

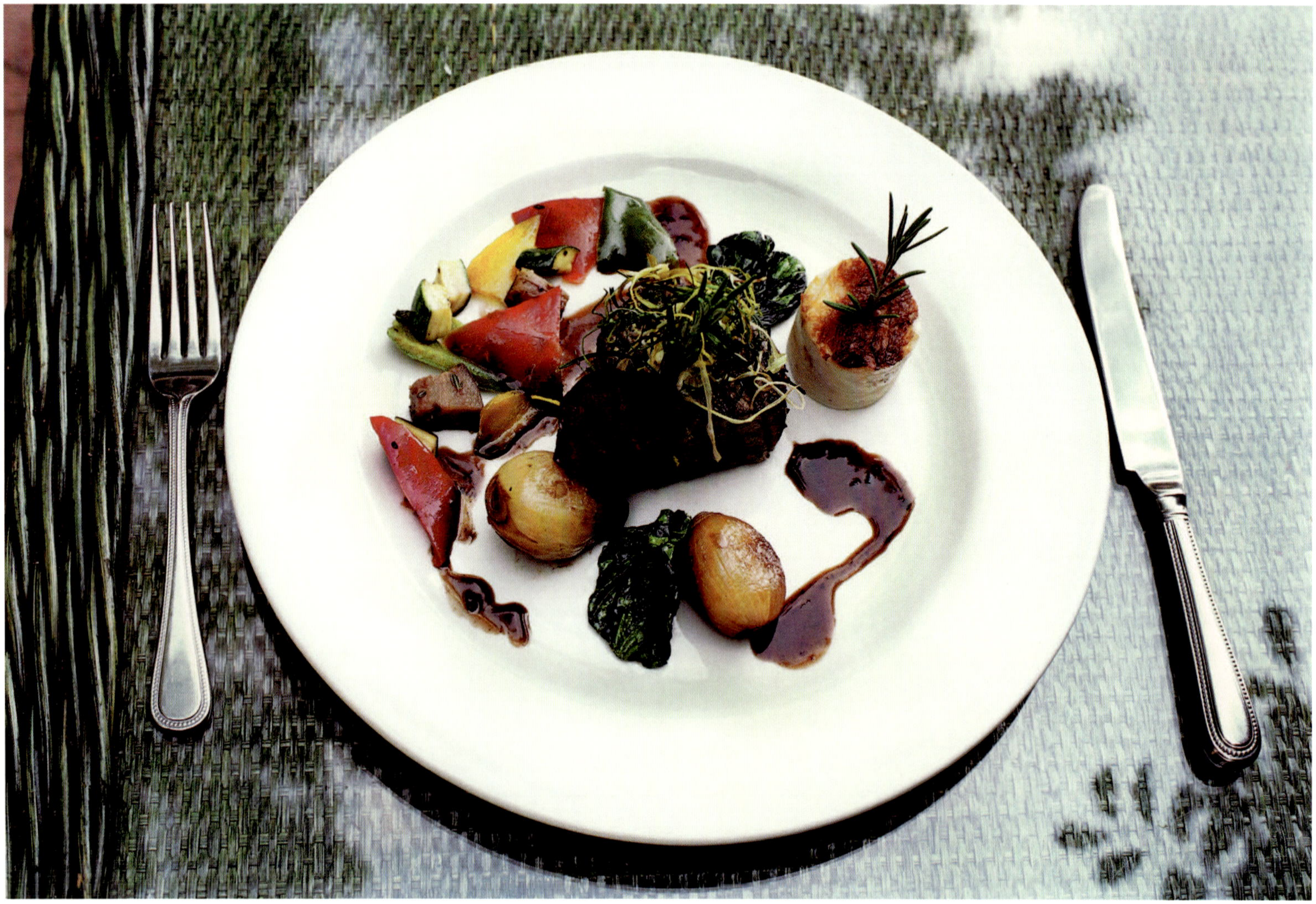

Fillet of Beef with Marrow Crust, Rosemary and Honey Sauce and Julienne Leeks

Serves 4

4 x 180 g beef fillets
50 ml rosemary, chopped
50 ml thyme, chopped
salt & pepper to taste
10 ml extra virgin olive oil

Marrow crust

120 g raw beef bone marrow
40 g white breadcrumbs
1 clove garlic, crushed
20 ml thyme, chopped
20 ml parsley, chopped
salt & pepper

Rosemary and honey sauce

1 litre beef stock
250 ml port
500 ml red wine
30 ml rosemary
125 ml honey
100 g refrigerated butter cut into 1 cm blocks
salt & pepper to taste

Deep-fried julienne leeks

2 leeks
vegetable oil for deep-frying

Preheat the oven to 160 °C.

Season the fillets with the herbs, salt and pepper. Heat the oil in a frying pan over a moderate heat and fry the fillets for 5 minutes on each side to seal in the meat juices. Set aside.

In the meantime, prepare the marrow crust by blending the bone marrow, breadcrumbs, garlic, thyme, parsley, salt and pepper in a food processor until smooth. Roll out the crust, approximately 1 cm thick, between 2 layers of greaseproof paper and refrigerate until needed.

To make the rosemary and honey sauce, add all the ingredients together and bring to the boil over a moderate heat. When the sauce reaches boiling point, reduce the heat and simmer for approximately 1 hour to reach a fairly thick consistency. Remove from the heat and set aside until ready to use. Just before serving, reheat the sauce and whisk in the chilled butter, one block at a time.

Prepare the leeks by cutting them into 5 cm bits. Slice the leek pieces in half lengthwise and then into very thin 1 mm strips to resemble matchsticks. Deep-fry in hot oil and drain on towelling paper.

When ready to serve, shape a piece of the marrow crust to resemble the top of the fillet and place it on the fillet, pressing it down to secure it. Repeat with the remaining fillets. Place in the oven for 5 minutes. When done, place the fillet in the centre of the plate and pour 30 ml of the sauce over the fillet.

Serve with potatoes and vegetables of your choice.

Garnish with deep-fried julienne leeks.

Suggested wine: Cabernet Sauvignon or Merlot

Kudu Medallions Rolled in Nuts with Redcurrant Jus and Potato Gratin

Serves 4

12 x 60 g kudu fillet medallions
salt & pepper to taste
45 ml basil pesto (page 41)
45 ml rosemary, chopped
100 ml roasted macadamia nuts, chopped
15 ml extra virgin olive oil
fresh basil leaves for garnish

Redcurrant jus

1 litre beef stock
500 ml red wine
100 ml raspberry vinegar
75 g redcurrants
200 ml port
100 g refrigerated butter cut into 1 cm blocks

Potato gratin

6 large potatoes, peeled and thinly sliced
salt & pepper
10 ml ground nutmeg
1 clove garlic, finely chopped
500 ml cream
60 ml grated Parmesan cheese

Preheat the oven to 160 °C.

Season each medallion and roll in the pesto, herbs and nuts. Heat the oil in a griddle pan over a moderate heat and fry the medallions for approximately 5 minutes on each side to seal in the meat juices. Set aside until ready to use.

To make the redcurrant jus, place all the ingredients, except the butter, in a saucepan. Reduce the sauce slowly over a low heat for 1 hour until a fairly thick consistency is reached. Remove from the heat and set aside until ready to use. When ready to serve, reheat the sauce and whisk in the chilled butter, one block at a time.

In the meantime, prepare the potato gratin. Layer the potato slices in an ovenproof dish. Combine the salt, pepper, nutmeg, garlic and cream and pour the mixture over the potato slices. Top with grated Parmesan. Bake for 45 minutes until soft and the Parmesan is crispy. Keep in the fridge until ready to use. Refrigerated potato gratin can be kept for up to 3 days. When ready to serve, reheat in the oven or a microwave.

To assemble the dish, cut out any preferred shape from the potato gratin and place it on the plate. Arrange the medallions around the gratin and drizzle the sauce over the kudu.

Garnish with fresh basil leaves.

Suggested wine: Shiraz

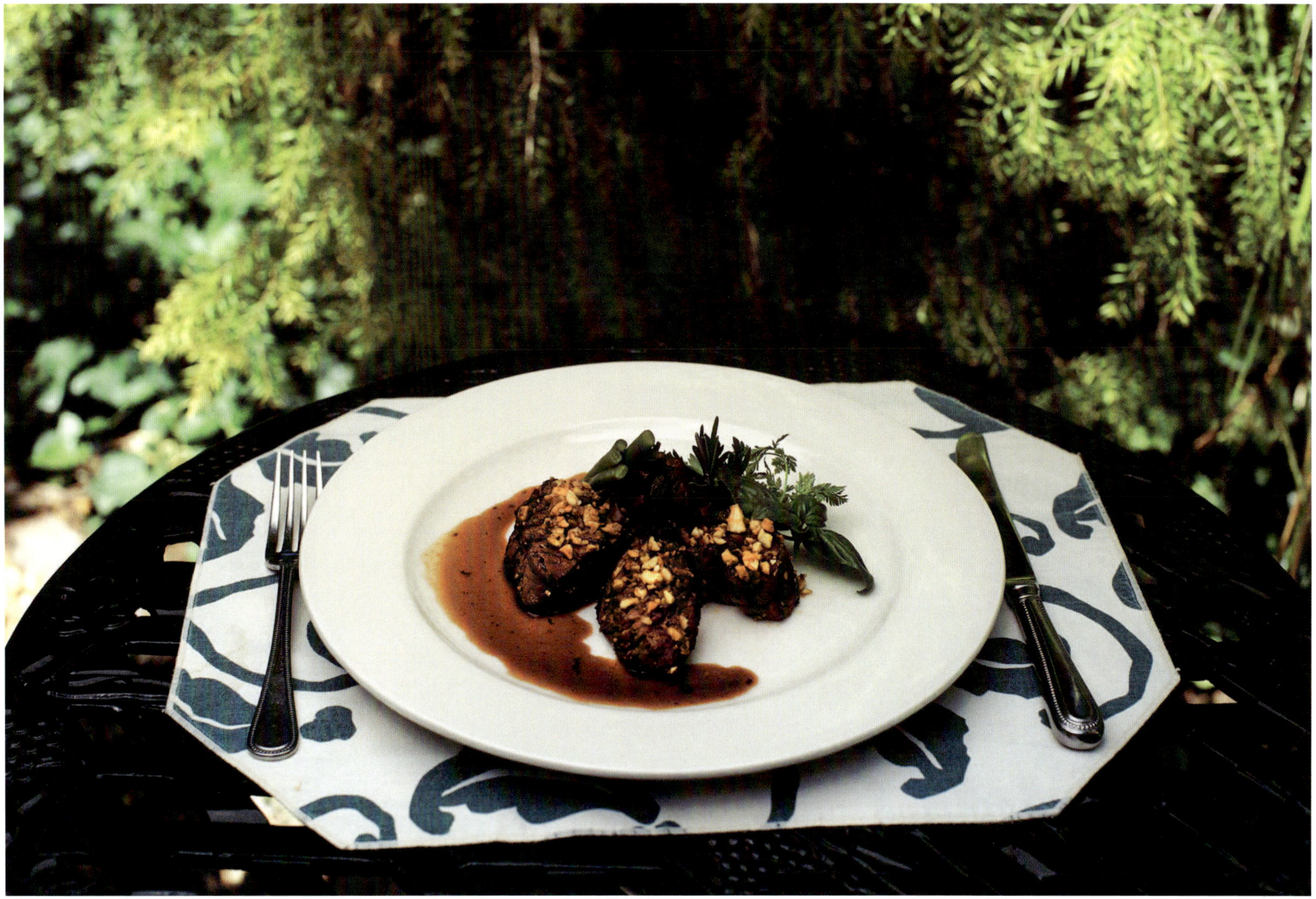

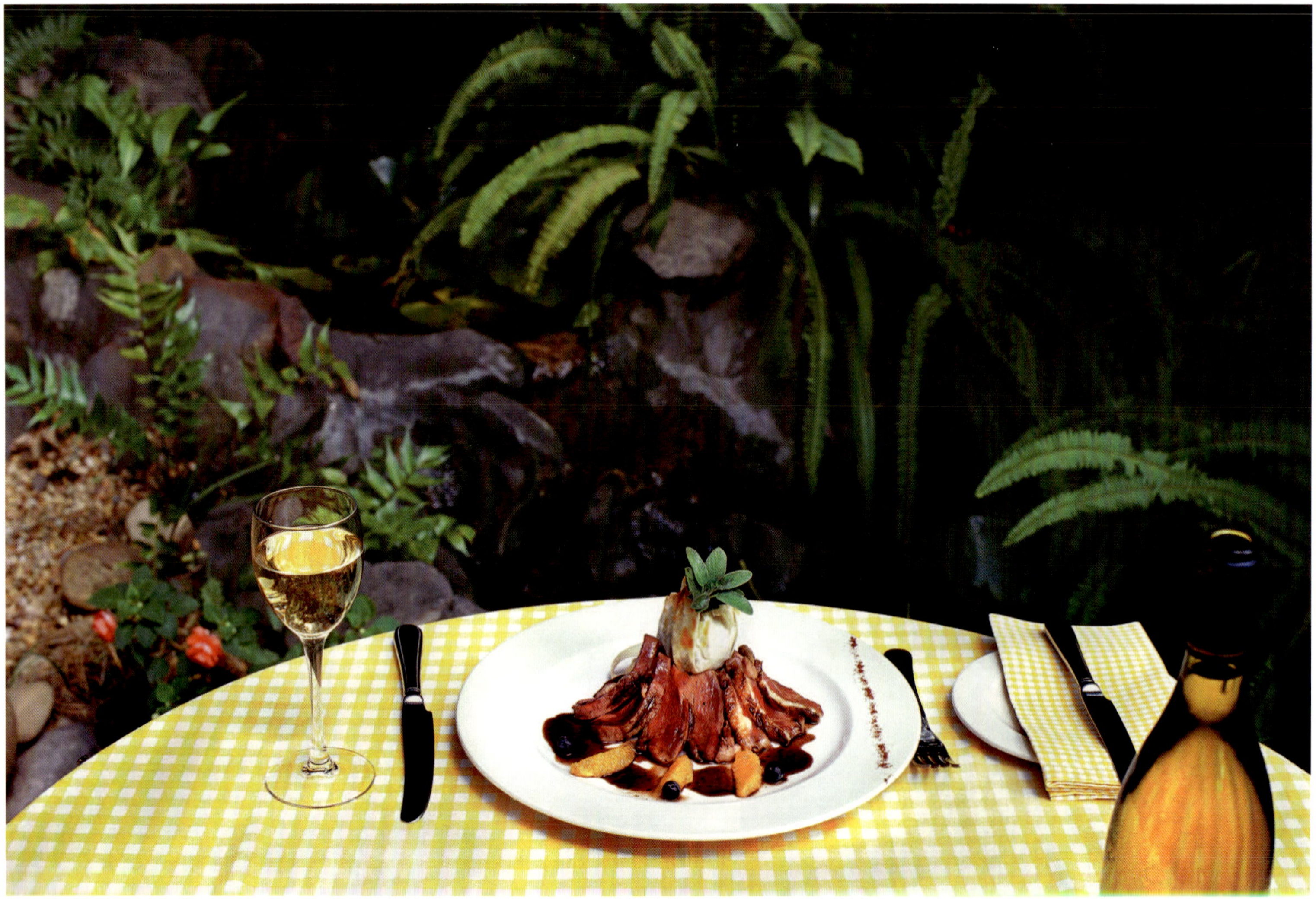

Orange Duck Magret with Duck Liver Parcels

Serves 4

4 x 180 g duck magret breasts
salt & pepper to taste
25 ml extra virgin olive oil
orange segments, blueberries and sage for garnish

Orange sauce

250 ml orange juice
500 ml chicken stock
50 ml Cointreau liqueur
20 ml fresh thyme, chopped
salt & pepper to taste

Duck liver parcels

200 g duck livers, roughly chopped
5 ml extra virgin olive oil
20 ml onion, chopped
1 clove garlic, chopped
10 ml thyme, chopped
15 ml brandy
salt & pepper
4 phyllo pastry sheets, buttered

Preheat the oven to 180 °C.

Season the duck breasts. Heat the oil in a saucepan and fry the duck over a moderate heat for 5 minutes on each side.

Combine all the ingredients for the orange sauce in a saucepan. Reduce the sauce over a moderate heat for 30 minutes until pouring consistency. Remove from the heat and strain through a sieve.

To make the duck liver parcels, pan-fry the duck livers with the onion, garlic and thyme over a moderate heat. Cook for 5 minutes. Flambé by pouring the brandy over the duck livers, heating it through, and setting it alight. When flames are extinguished, season to taste and cool.

Spoon the filling into four phyllo pastry parcels. Bake the parcels for 5 minutes.

When ready to serve, place the duck breasts in the oven with the parcels for 5 minutes. Remove from the oven and rest for 3 minutes. Cut each duck breast into 5 slices and arrange on a plate. Place the parcel on top and drizzle the sauce over the duck. Serve with tagliatelle or potatoes.

Garnish with fresh orange segments, blueberries and sage.

Suggested wine: Cabernet Sauvignon

Serves 4

3 Peking duck legs
250 g coarse salt
500 ml lard
500 g pumpkin, peeled and diced
2 onions, chopped
30 ml thyme
15 ml extra virgin olive oil
250 ml risotto rice
125 ml white wine
500 ml chicken stock
salt & pepper
30 ml chopped chives for garnish

Parmesan tuiles

60 ml grated Parmesan cheese
ground black pepper

Duck and Pumpkin Risotto

Preheat the oven to 180 °C.

Cover the duck legs in coarse salt and leave to stand at room temperature for 1 hour. Wash off the salt. In a heavy-based saucepan, slowly cook the duck in the lard over a low heat for approximately 2 hours. Remove the duck legs from the fat and shred the meat with 2 forks. Reserve a little of the fat, approximately 50 ml.

Roast the pumpkin, 1 chopped onion and thyme in the oven for 35 minutes.

Place the second chopped onion, oil and risotto rice in a pot. Slowly heat the mixture, then add the wine and chicken stock. Stir continuously until *al dente*. Add the extra water if necessary. Cook for approximately 10 minutes. Season to taste.

To make the Parmesan tuiles, spoon 4 mounds of Parmesan cheese on a baking tray lined with greaseproof paper. Grill for 3 minutes until brown and crispy. Take care not to burn the Parmesan cheese. Remove from under the grill and sprinkle with freshly ground black pepper.

When ready to serve, mix the reserved fat with the shredded duck. Gently mix together the pumpkin, shredded duck and risotto. Keep back some of the shredded duck to use as garnish. Serve topped with Parmesan tuile and chopped chives.

Suggested wine: Pinot Noir

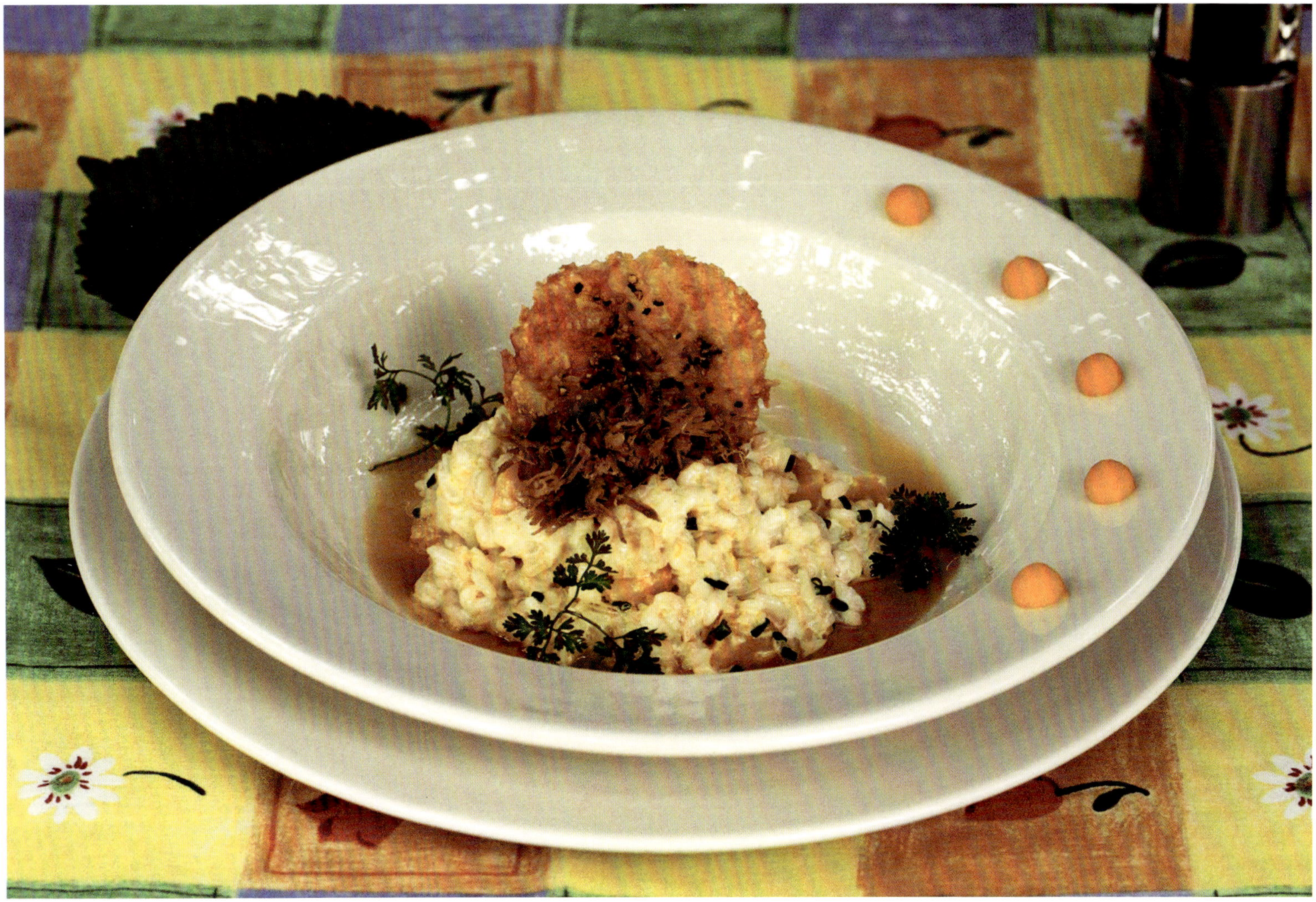

Food is an important part of a balanced diet.

FRAN LEBOWITZ

Desserts

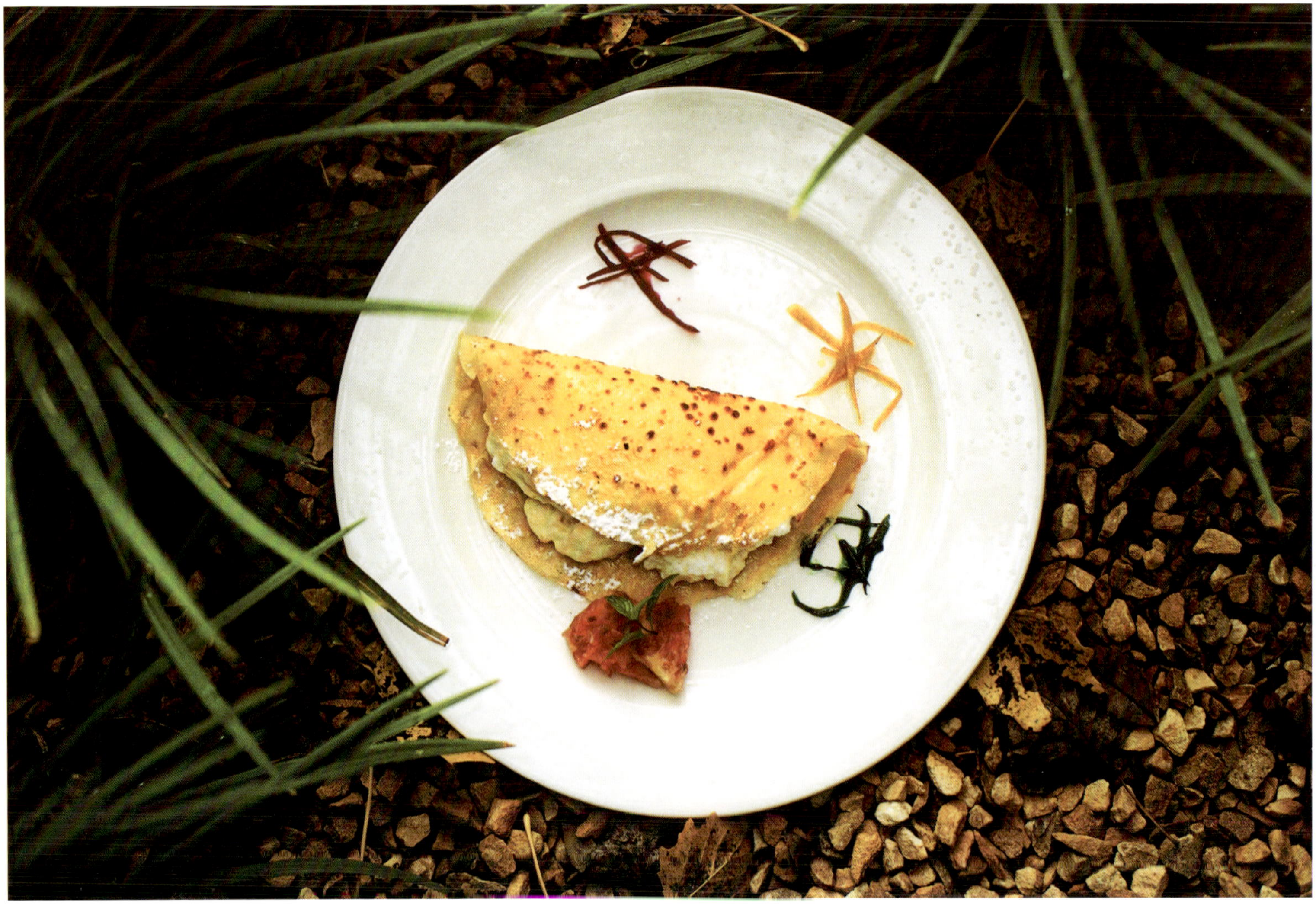

Serves 4

100 g flour
500 ml milk
50 ml melted butter
2 eggs
1 egg yolk
zest of 1 orange
pinch of salt
vegetable oil for frying

Orange crème patisserie

125 ml milk
125 ml orange juice
35 g cake flour
75 g sugar
2 egg yolks
zest of 1 orange
2 egg whites
60 ml Mandarin Napoleon (liqueur)
icing sugar for dusting
orange segments for garnish

Orange Crêpe Soufflé

Preheat the oven to 180 °C.

First prepare the crêpes by sifting the flour into a bowl and adding the milk, butter, eggs, egg yolk, orange zest and salt. Whisk until the batter is smooth. Let it rest for 30 minutes at room temperature.

Heat a crêpe pan with 5 ml oil. When the base is heated through, pour off the excess oil. With a soup ladle, pour in approximately 50 ml of the batter. Rotate the pan to spread the batter and lightly coat the base. The thinner the crêpe, the better. Cook each crêpe until golden brown on both sides. Stack the finished crêpes on top of one another and keep them in the fridge.

To prepare the crème patisserie, heat the milk and orange juice in a saucepan over a low heat to just below boiling point. Remove the mixture from the heat and add the flour, sugar, egg yolks and orange zest. Cook the mixture in a double boiler over a low heat until the flour has cooked and the crème patisserie has thickened.

Just before serving, whisk 2 egg whites until they form firm peaks. Gently fold the crème patisserie into the egg white.

Place a spoonful of the mixture on each crêpe. Fold the crêpes in half and place them on a baking tray. Bake in the oven for 8 minutes.

When ready to serve, top the crêpes with icing sugar and pour over the Mandarin Napoleon.

Garnish with orange segments.

Layered Hazelnut Meringues with Lemon Curd and Berry Coulis

Serves 6

6 egg whites
375 g castor sugar
125 g roasted hazelnuts, chopped
zest of one orange for garnish
mint leaves for garnish

Lemon curd

juice of 9 lemons
30 g corn flour
6 eggs
515 g castor sugar
grated rind of 2 lemons
45 g unsalted butter

Berry coulis

100 g fresh mixed berries
50 g sugar
150 ml water

Preheat the oven to 100 °C.

To make the meringues, whisk 2 egg whites until they form firm peaks. Gradually add the sugar while continuing to whisk the egg white. When the mixture is stiff and glossy, fold in the hazelnuts.

Pipe 18 rounds (approximately 6 cm in diameter) of the mixture onto a baking tray lined with greaseproof paper. Place in the oven for 1 hour. Turn off the heat and leave the meringues to cool in the oven until completely dry.

Meanwhile, prepare the lemon curd by adding the lemon juice to the corn flour to form a paste. Combine the corn flour and lemon paste with the eggs, castor sugar and lemon rind and heat in a double boiler. Stir continuously for approximately 10 minutes until the mixture has thickened. Remove from the heat and whisk in the butter. Set the lemon curd aside to cool.

Make the coulis by bringing the berries, sugar and water to the boil. Lower the temperature and simmer until the sauce thickens. The desired consistency is reached when the sauce visibly coats the back of a spoon and does not fall off. Strain the mixture through a sieve and set aside to cool.

When ready to serve, arrange alternate layers of the meringue disks and the lemon curd, finishing with a meringue disc.

Garnish with berry coulis, orange zest and mint leaves.

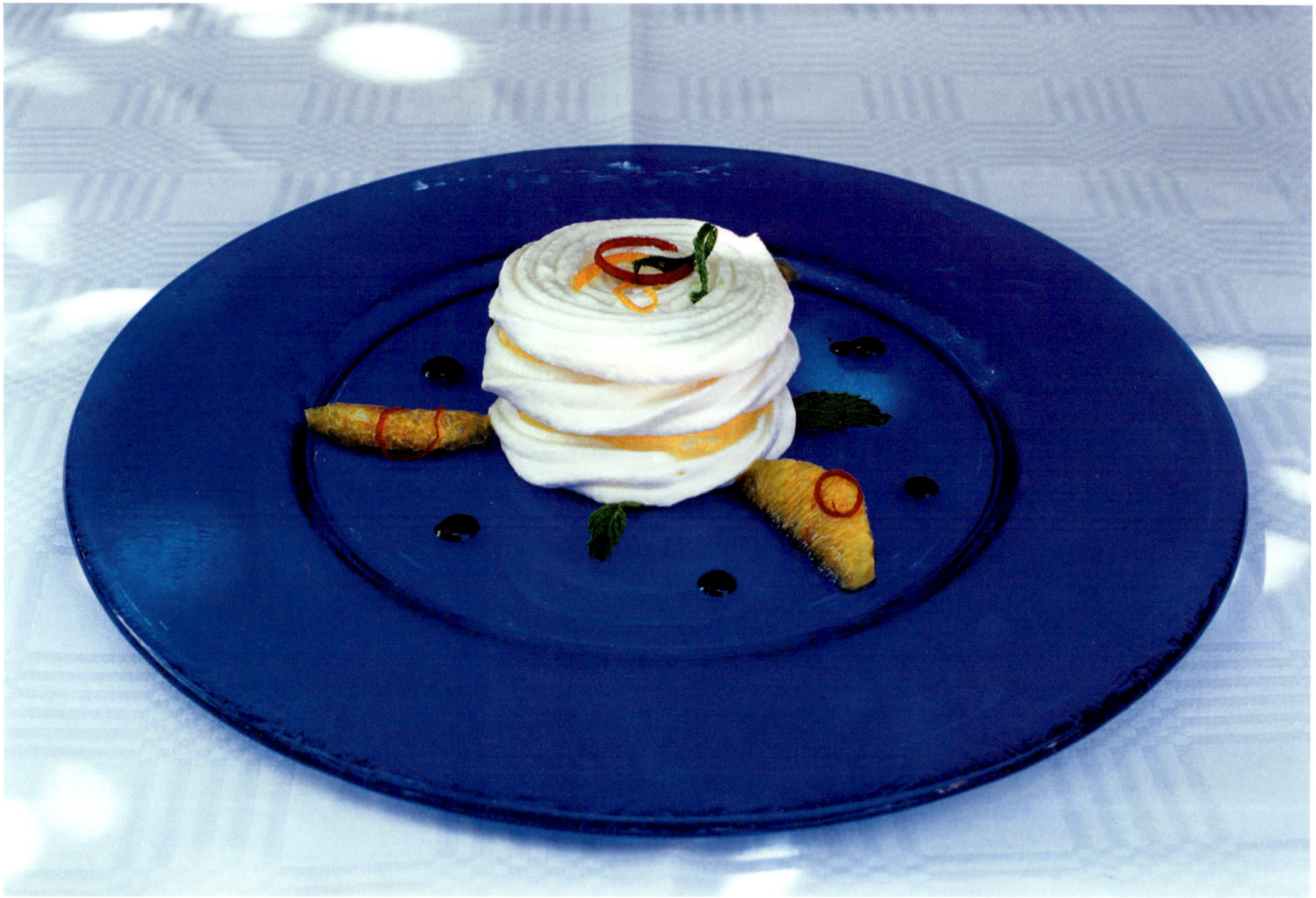

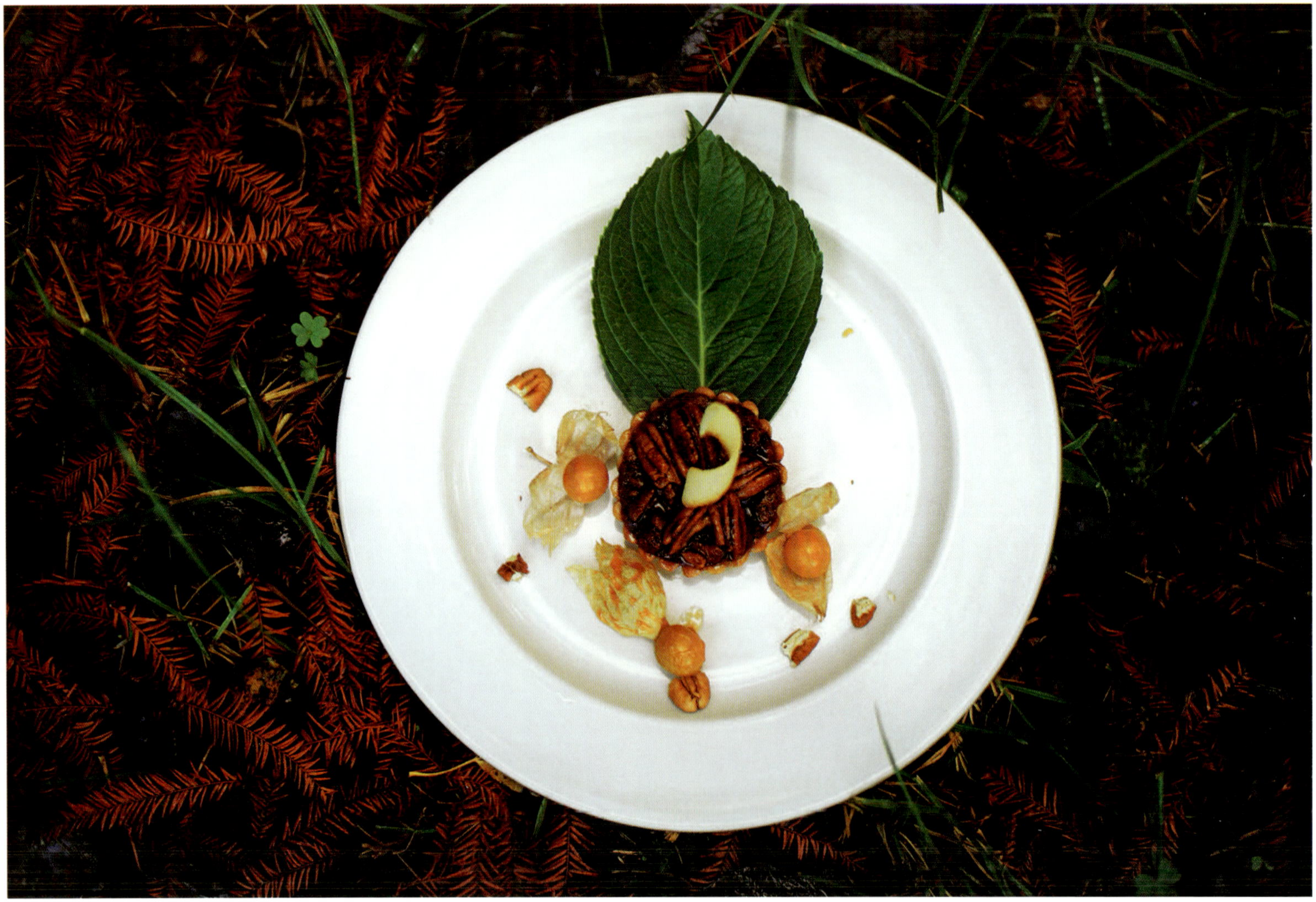

Serves 6

450 g cake flour
225 g unsalted butter
150 g sugar
4 egg yolks
30 ml iced water
100 ml melted apricot jam
cream or ice cream

Filling

2 eggs, beaten
125 g brown sugar
125 ml liquid glucose (available in speciality stores)
25 ml melted unsalted butter
250 ml pecan nuts
2.5 ml vanilla essence

Pecan Nut Pie

Preheat the oven to 180 °C.

To make the pie crust, mix the flour, butter, sugar and egg yolks with a wooden spoon. Add the iced water and knead the mixture into a dough. Cover and leave to rest in the fridge for 20 minutes.

Prepare the filling by mixing the eggs, sugar and glucose with the melted butter. Add the pecan nuts and vanilla essence.

Remove the dough from the fridge. Roll the dough to 3 mm thickness. Then line a shallow ovenproof tart dish (25 cm in diameter) with the dough. Pour the filling into the tart dish and bake for 20 minutes. Remove from the oven and glaze with the melted apricot jam. Slice into 6 portions.

Serve hot, with cream or ice cream.

Hot Chocolate Fondant

Serves 6

225 g dark chocolate (with 70% cocoa)*
225 g unsalted butter
9 eggs
62.5 g castor sugar
5 ml baking powder
50 g cake flour
20 ml very strong coffee or brewed espresso
fresh mixed berries for garnish

Preheat the oven to 180 °C.

Melt the chocolate and butter in a double boiler. Beat the eggs and sugar until light in colour and fluffy. Gradually add this mixture to the melted chocolate and butter mixture. Using a metal spoon, fold in the baking powder, flour and coffee.

Pour the mixture into 6 buttered and floured fondant moulds and bake for 10–12 minutes. Remove from the oven. The middle of the fondants should still be liquid.

Carefully transfer each mould to a plate, using a broad spatula. Separate the fondant from the mould with the tip of a sharp knife. Gently slide the mould over the top of the fondant.

Serve with fresh berries.

* Choose a dark chocolate with a 70% cocoa content.

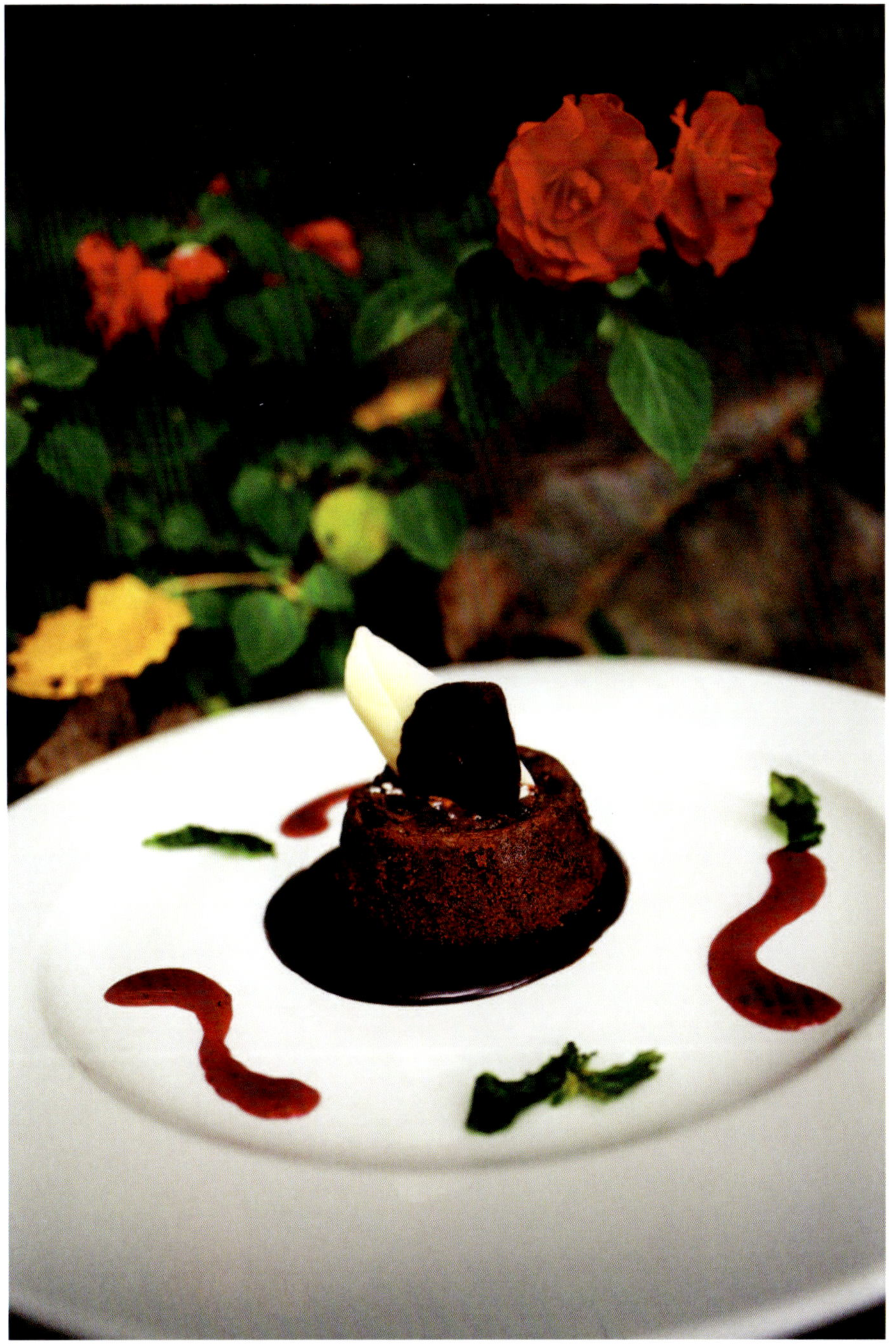

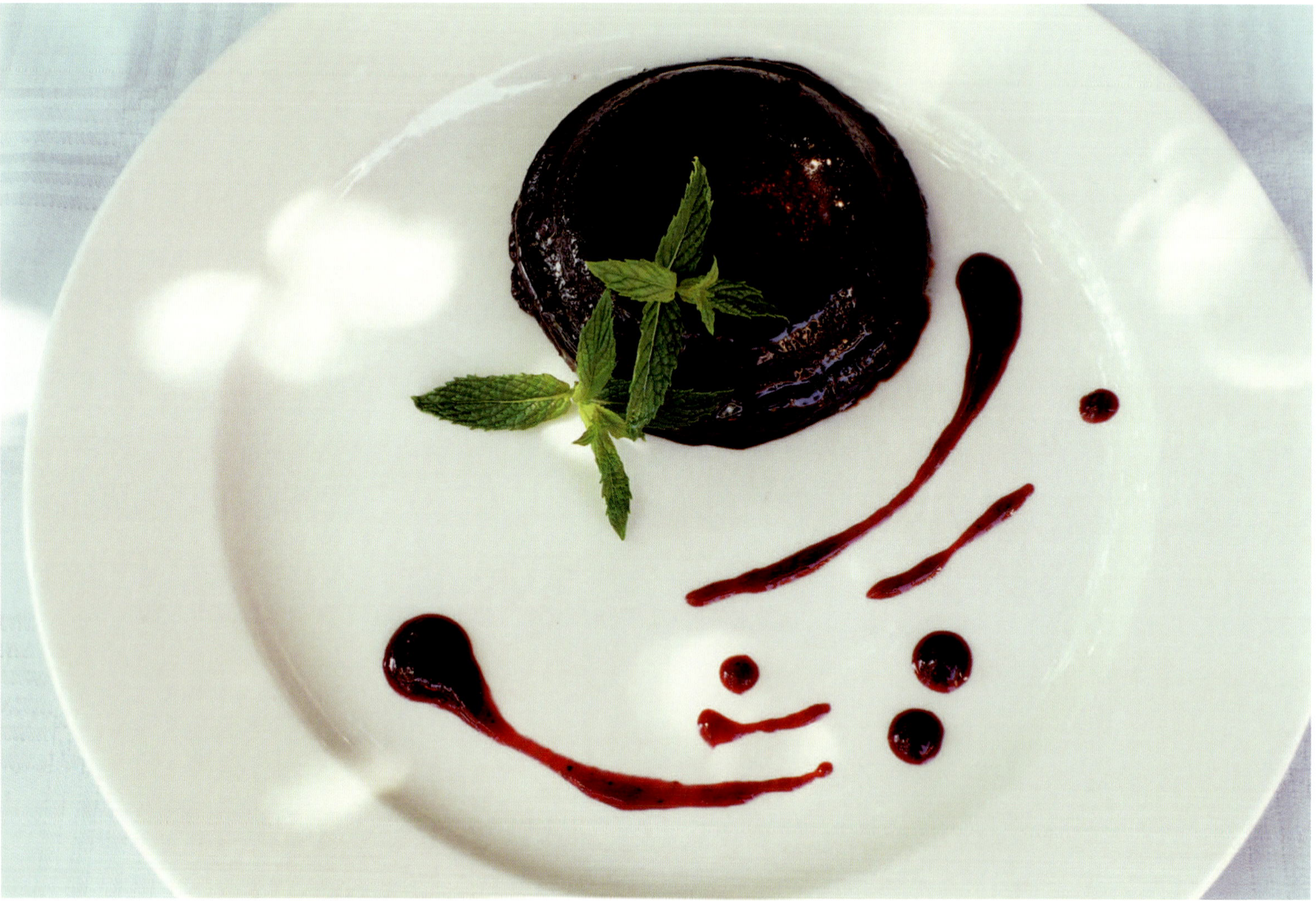

Serves 4

350 g dark chocolate (with 70% cocoa)*
100 g unsalted butter
8 eggs
50 g castor sugar
30 ml strong coffee
60 ml flour
30 ml baking powder
Drambuie ganache (page 97)
fresh raspberries for garnish
mint leaves for garnish

Mames Cake

Preheat the oven to 180 °C.

Melt the chocolate and butter in a double boiler over a low heat. Cream the eggs, sugar and coffee together until they are well combined, then stir in the melted chocolate mixture.

Sift the flour and baking powder together. Using a metal spoon, gently stir it into the batter. Pour the mixture into 4 buttered moulds and bake for 12 minutes.

Just before serving, remove the cakes from the moulds and spoon the ganache over each cake.

Garnish with fresh raspberries and mint leaves.

* Choose a dark chocolate with a 70% cocoa content.

Serves 6

350 g cake flour
4 egg yolks
2 eggs
pinch of salt
25 ml vegetable oil
15 ml cocoa powder
50 g castor sugar
1 egg white
berry coulis for garnish (page 82)

Chocolate mousse filling

250 g dark chocolate
1 egg
1 egg yolk
10 g icing sugar

Chocolate Ravioli

Prepare the pasta dough by mixing the flour, egg yolks, eggs, salt, oil, cocoa powder and castor sugar in a food processor until smooth. Leave to rest in the fridge for 30 minutes.

Using a pasta machine, roll the chocolate dough to the desired thickness (about 1 mm). We recommend you set your machine to no. 5.

To make the chocolate mousse filling, melt the chocolate in a double boiler. Cream the egg, egg yolk and icing sugar together until they are well combined. Gently fold the egg mixture into the melted chocolate. Keep the chocolate mousse in the fridge until needed.

Cut the dough into 6 rounds (6 cm in diameter) and brush them with the egg white. Place 1 teaspoon of the mousse filling in the centre of each round. Gently fold the pastry over and press the edges down with the teeth of a fork to seal in the filling.

Heat a pot of water to just below boiling point. Take care not to boil the water. Place the ravioli in the hot water and cook for 4 minutes. Remove the ravioli with a sieve or slotted spoon, and serve hot.

Garnish with berry coulis.

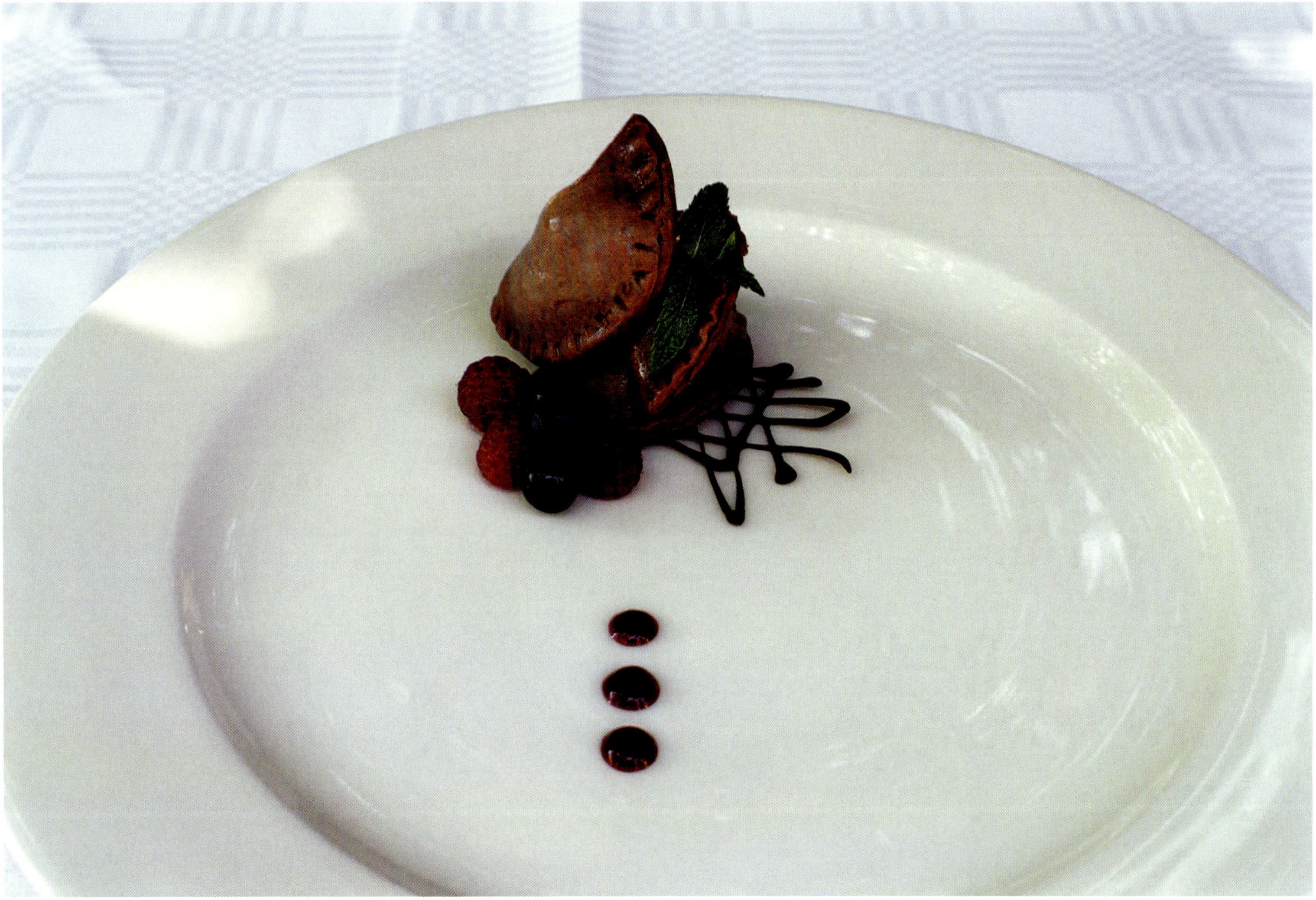

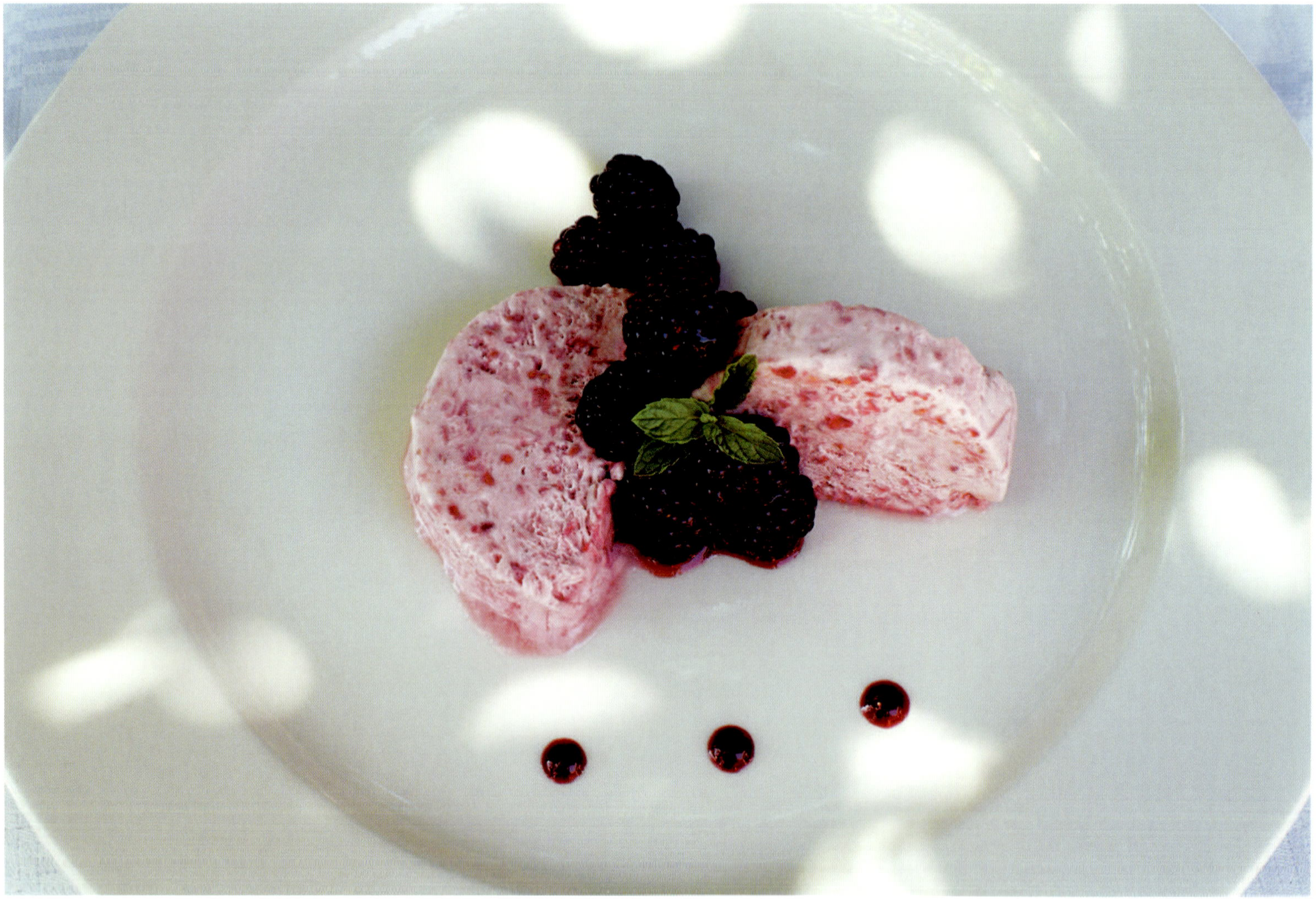

Serves 4

4 egg yolks
175 g sugar
100 g fresh mixed berries
150 g cream, whipped

Minted berries

40 ml chopped mint
40 g fresh mixed berries
10 ml Crème de Cassis liqueur
spearmint leaves for garnish

Hot Minted Berry Parfait

Cream the egg yolks and 125 g of sugar together in a double boiler over a low heat until the sugar has dissolved and the mixture is thick and light in colour. In a saucepan, cook the mixed berries with the remaining sugar for approximately 10 minutes. Add the berry mixture to the egg yolk mixture. Leave to cool.

Whip the cream until it holds its shape. Gently fold the cream into the egg and berry mixture, then pour it into 6 moulds and freeze for 6 hours.

Just before serving, prepare the minted berries by heating the berries, Crème de Cassis and chopped mint in a saucepan. Remove the parfait from the moulds and place on serving plates. Pour the hot minted berries over the cold parfait. Serve immediately.

Garnish with fresh spearmint leaves.

Serves 4

4 pears, peeled
500 ml red wine
250 ml water
250 g sugar
2 star anise
2 cinnamon sticks
1 vanilla pod
200 g Stilton cheese

Grilled Pears with Stilton Cheese

In a saucepan, bring the red wine, water, sugar, spices and vanilla pod to the boil and lower the heat. Add the pears and cook for approximately 10 minutes until they are soft but firm. Leave the pears to marinate in the syrup for 12 hours until rich-red in colour. Drain the pears and keep the syrup.

When ready to serve, cut the pears in half and remove their cores. Place them rounded side up on serving plates. Top with the Stilton cheese. Place the pears under a grill until the cheese melts.

In the meantime, reduce the syrup to a pouring consistency. Serve the pears hot, topped with the sauce.

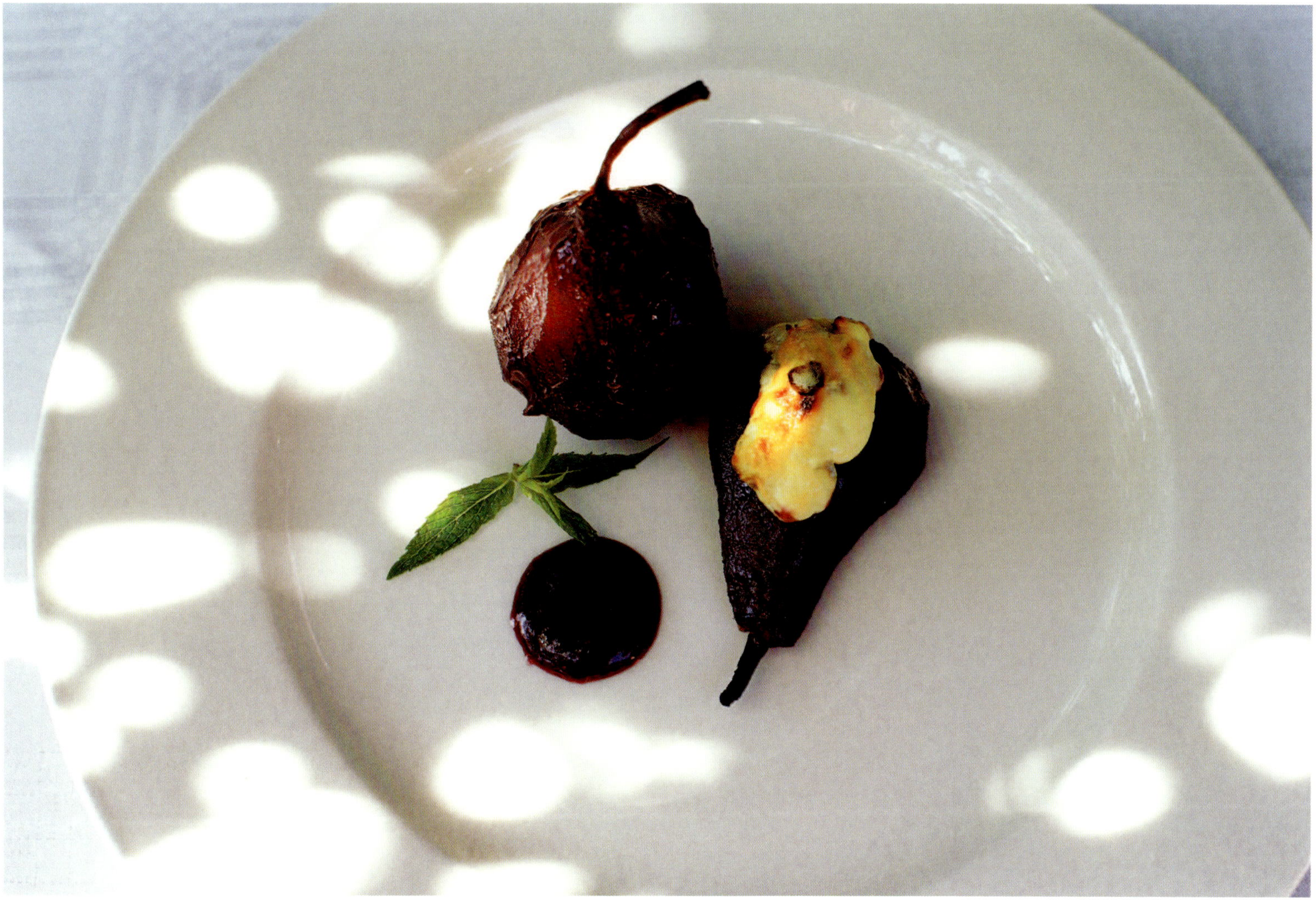

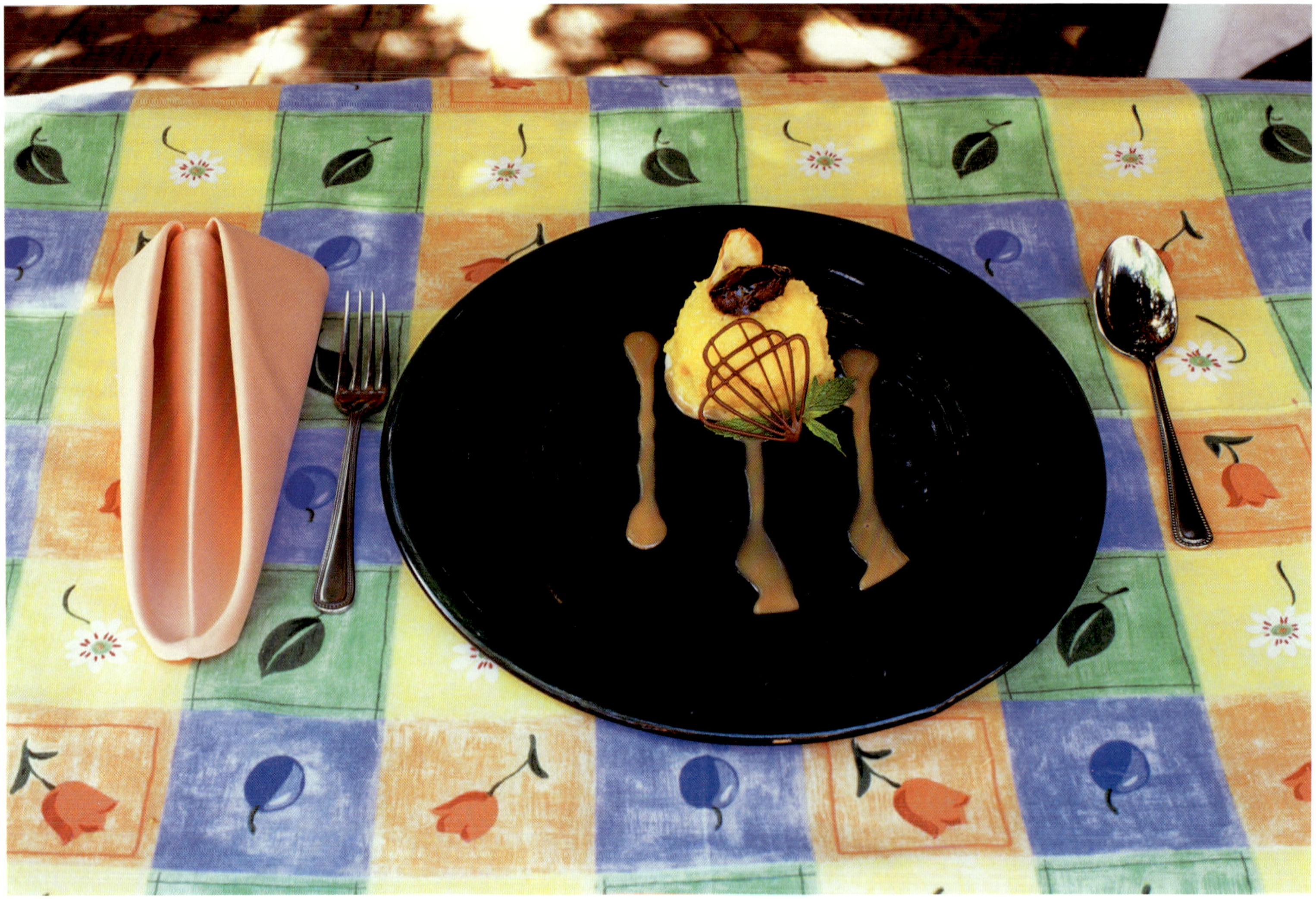

Serves 6

750 g sweet potato, with skins
150 g unsalted butter
200 g castor sugar
10 ml dark rum
3 eggs

Drambuie ganache

60 ml cream
170 g dark chocolate, roughly chopped
50 g unsalted butter
2 egg yolks
15 ml Drambuie whisky

Sweet potato chips

1 sweet potato
icing sugar for dusting

Creole Sweet Potato Cake

Preheat the oven to 200 °C.

Bake the sweet potatoes for about 1 hour in the oven. Remove them from the oven and peel their skins. Mash the sweet potato until smooth.

Cream the butter, sugar and rum together until the mixture is light in colour. Add the eggs one at a time.

Fold the mashed sweet potato into the butter mixture. Pour the mixture into buttered ramekins and cook them in a water bath (bain-marie). To make the bain-marie, place the ramekins in a shallow roasting pan half filled with warm water so that they are surrounded with gentle heat. Then cover the pan with tin foil and bake for 1 hour.

Prepare the ganache by heating the cream in a saucepan. Just before it reaches boiling point, remove it from the heat. Whisk in the chocolate, butter, egg yolks and Drambuie. Stir the mixture until the ingredients are well combined and the sauce is thick and rich in colour. Keep refrigerated until needed.

To make the sweet potato chips, cut the sweet potato into thin slices and dust with the icing sugar. Place them on a baking tray in a cool oven. Bake for 30 minutes at 100 °C until dry and crispy.

When ready to serve, remove the cakes from the ramekins and cover each one with the Drambuie ganache.

Garnish with sweet potato chips.

Serves 4

5 Granny Smith apples, peeled and diced
60 g brown sugar
1 star anise
1 vanilla pod
6 preserved figs, roughly chopped
4 phyllo pastry sheets, buttered
1 x 410 g tin of baby apples for garnish
fresh mint leaves for garnish

Ginger mascarpone

40 ml ginger preserve, chopped
200 ml mascarpone cheese

Fig and Apple Samoosas

Preheat the oven to 180 °C.

In a saucepan, cook the apples, sugar, star anise and vanilla pod over a low heat until the apple pieces are soft. Remove from the heat and add the figs. Remove the star anise and vanilla pod. Set aside to cool.

To make the ginger mascarpone, mix together the ginger preserve and mascarpone cheese. Set aside.

To make the samoosas, layer the 4 pastry sheets one on top of the other. Cut the pastry sheets vertically to form four long strips. Divide the fig mixture into 4 equal parts and spoon onto the bottom half of each pastry strip. Fold each strip into a triangle to form a samoosa shape, ensuring that the filling is sealed in. Bake the samoosas for 10 minutes until brown.

Cut each samoosa diagonally and serve with ginger mascarpone.

Garnish with baby apples and fresh mint leaves.

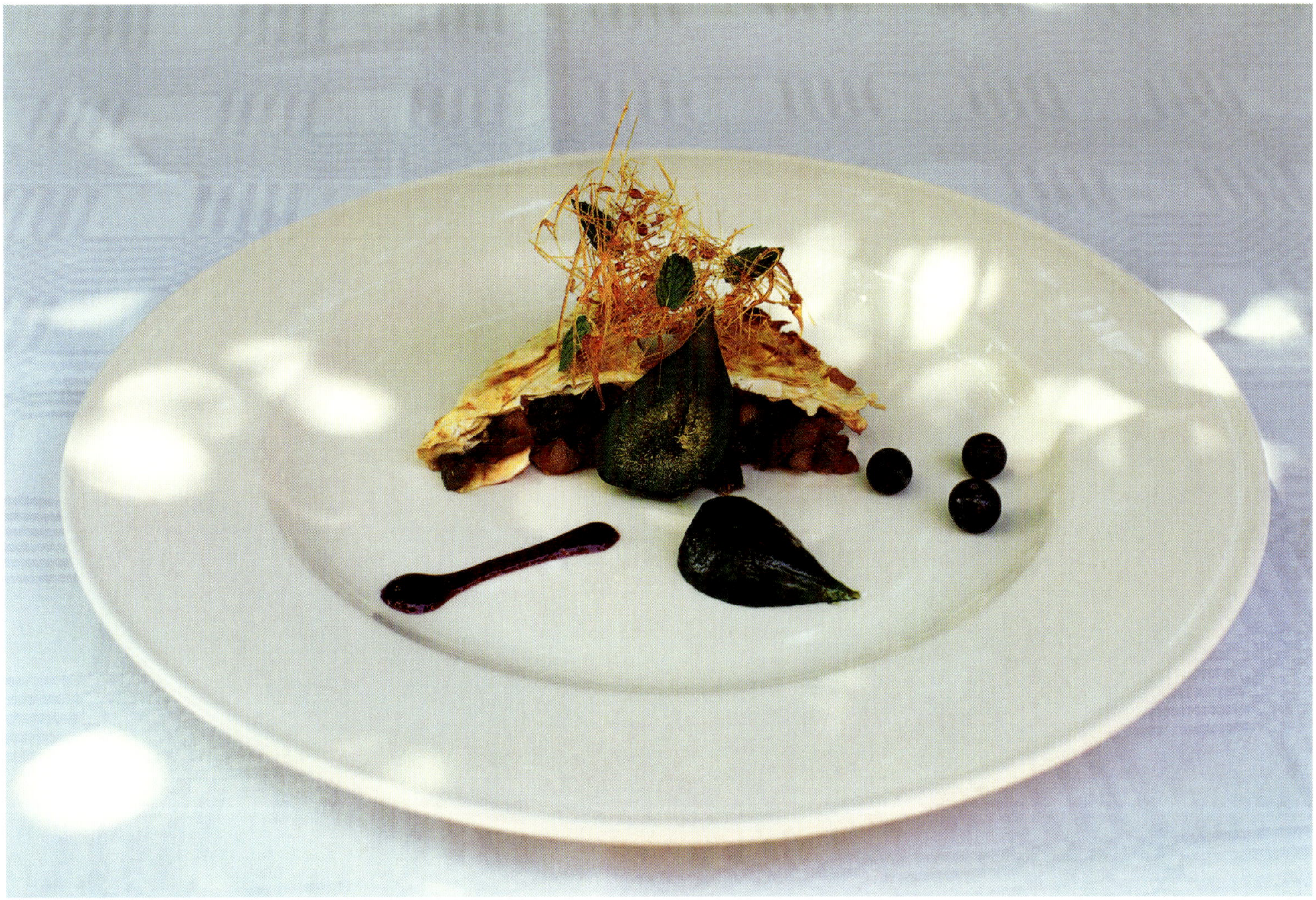

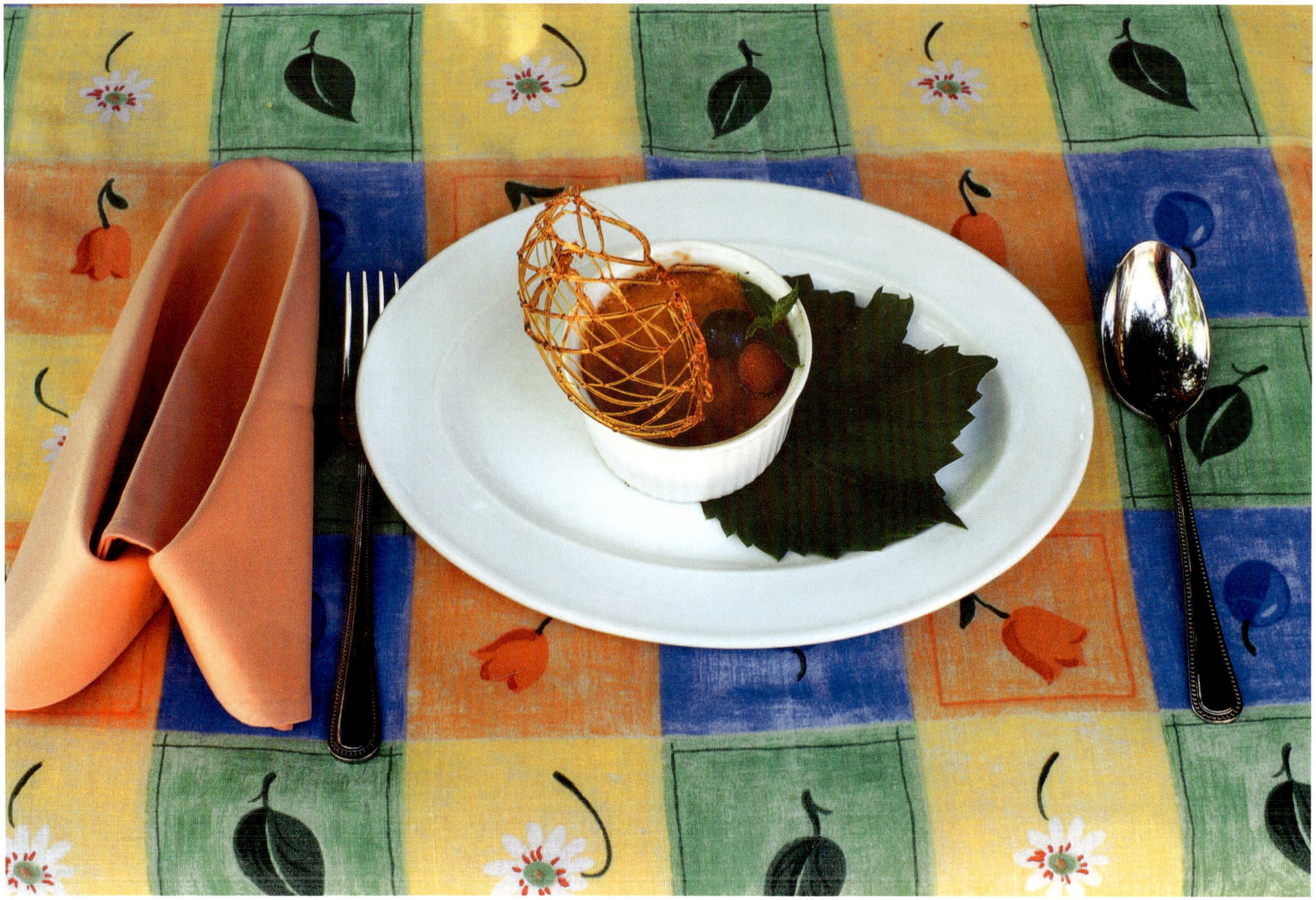

Crème Brûlée

Serves 4

8 egg yolks
100 g castor sugar
500 ml cream
1 vanilla pod
2.5 ml vanilla essence
20 g brown sugar for topping
seasonal fruit for garnish

Preheat the oven to 150 °C.

Beat the egg yolks and castor sugar together in a double boiler. Remove from the heat.

Cut the vanilla pod lengthwise with a sharp knife and scrape out the seeds. In a saucepan, heat the cream, vanilla pod and seeds and vanilla essence to just below boiling point. Remove from the heat and take out the vanilla pod. Gently fold the yolk and sugar mixture into the hot cream until well blended.

Pour the custard into 4 ramekins and bake them in a water bath (bain-marie). To make the bain-marie, place the ramekins in a shallow roasting pan half filled with warm water so that they are surrounded with gentle heat. Cover the pan with tin foil and bake for approximately 25 minutes in the oven until the custard has set. Remove from the oven and refrigerate.

When ready to serve, sprinkle 5 g of brown sugar over each custard. Caramelise the sugar with a small culinary blowtorch. If you do not have a blowtorch, you can broil the custards by placing the ramekins on ice under the grill for approximately 1 minute until the sugar turns brown.

Garnish with fresh seasonal fruit.

Serves 6

1 x 250 g packet sponge finger biscuits
50 ml strong coffee or brewed espresso
30 ml Kahlua
3 egg yolks
100 g castor sugar
250 g mascarpone cheese
250 ml cream, whipped
2 gelatine leaves
cocoa powder
coffee beans for garnish

Chocolate sauce

125 g castor sugar
50 g cocoa powder
100 ml cream
30 ml water

Tuiles

125 g castor sugar
75 g cake flour
2 eggs
pinch of salt
30 ml melted butter

Tiramisu

Stir together the coffee and Kahlua in a shallow bowl. Sprinkle the coffee beans over the biscuits. Remove the biscuits and arrange them in single layers on the bottom of 6 ring moulds (5–6 cm in diameter).

In a bowl, whisk the egg yolks and sugar until thick and creamy. Add the mascarpone and mix well. Whisk the cream into the mixture.

Soak the gelatine leaves in cold water for 5 minutes. Squeeze the excess liquid out of the gelatine. Spoon 30 ml of the tiramisu mixture into a pan and heat it through. Add the gelatine, allowing it to melt. Take care not to overheat the gelatine.

Gently mix the gelatine with the tiramisu mixture and pour it into the moulds. Refrigerate for about 2.5 hours until the tiramisu has set.

Meanwhile, prepare the tuiles by whisking together the castor sugar, flour, eggs, salt and butter. Leave to rest for 30 minutes. Pipe the mixture into long strips onto a greaseproof baking tray. Bake in a very hot oven (220 °C) for 4 minutes until the edges are golden brown. Remove from the oven. Twirl each strip around a wooden spoon to create a spiral shape.

To make the chocolate sauce, place the castor sugar, cocoa powder, cream and water in a saucepan. Gently cook the sauce over a low heat until it thickens to pouring consistency. Pass the sauce through a sieve. Set aside.

Remove the tiramisu from the moulds. Dust a little cocoa powder over the top and garnish with coffee beans. Serve with tuiles and chocolate sauce spooned onto the serving plates.

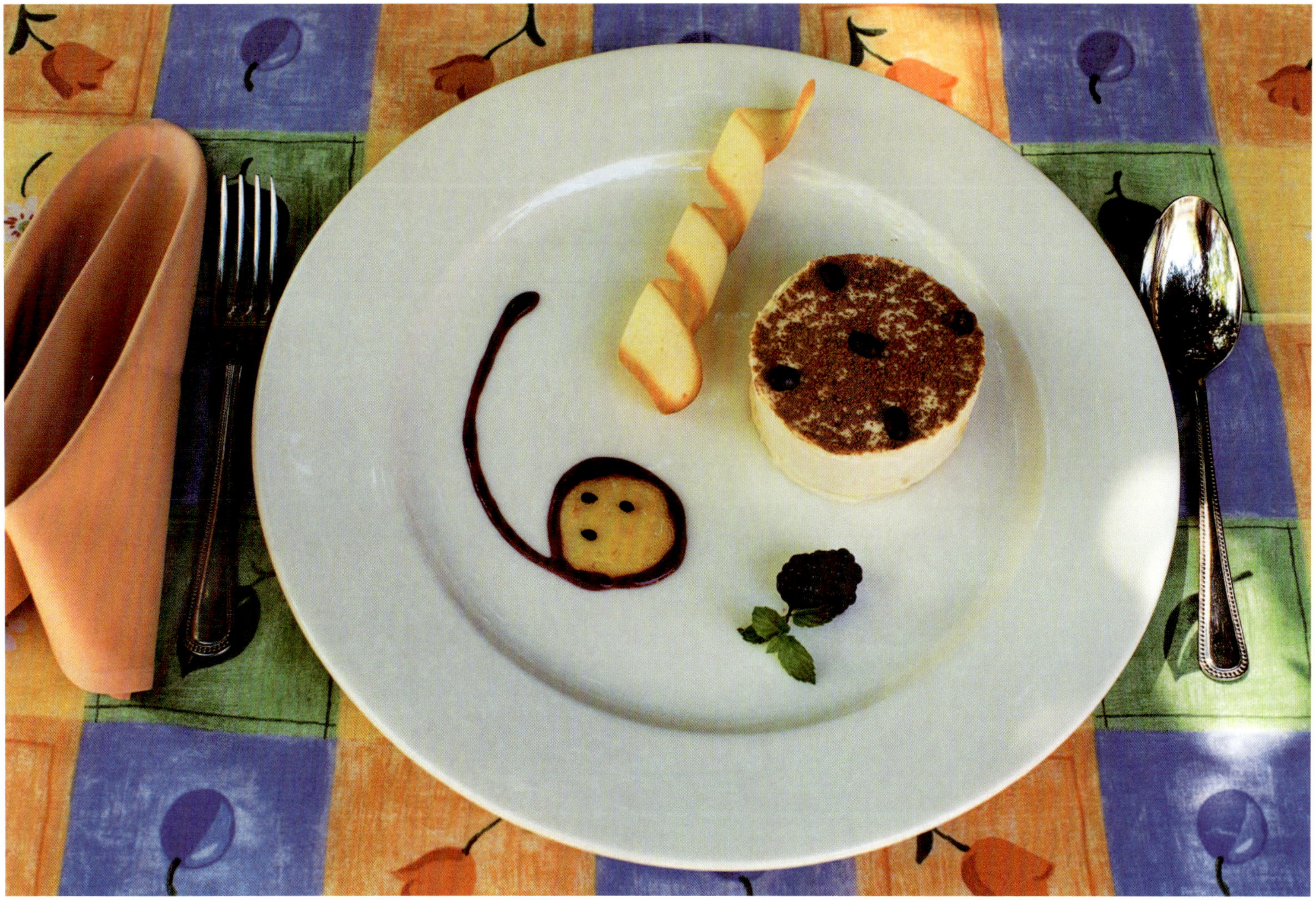

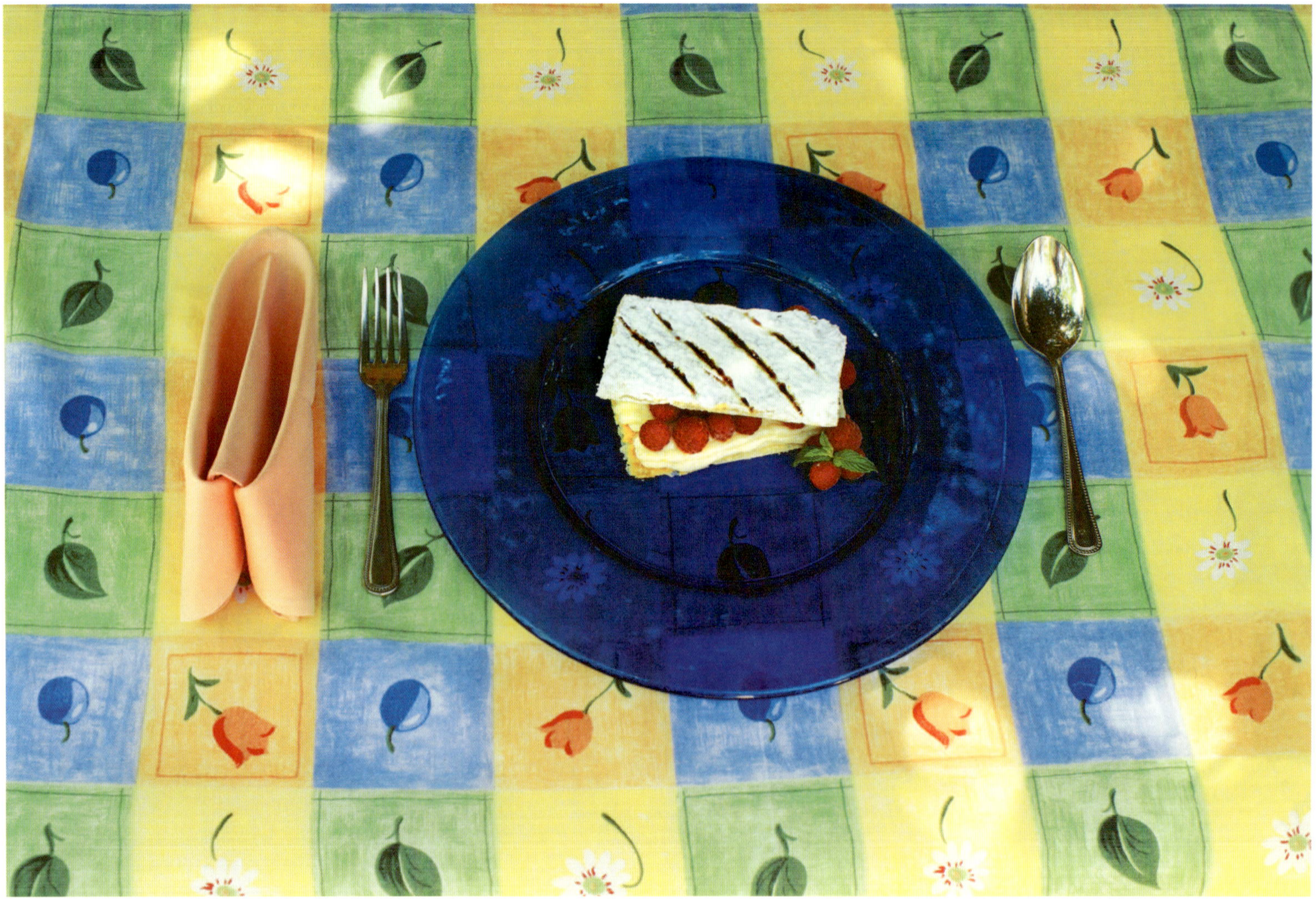

Serves 4

280 g puff pastry
15 ml melted butter
icing sugar for dusting
200 g fresh mixed berries
fresh mint for garnish

Vanilla crème patisserie

250 ml milk
60 g sugar
½ vanilla pod
35 g flour
2 egg yolks

Raspberry coulis

100 g fresh raspberries
60 g sugar
125 ml water

Berry Mille Feuille

Preheat the oven to 220 °C.

Roll out the puff pastry into a thin square shape. Cut it into 12 sheets of 10 cm x 6 cm (3 sheets per portion). Brush each sheet of pastry with the melted butter. Place the pastry on a greased baking tray and bake for approximately 10 minutes until golden brown. Remove from the oven and dust the pastry shapes with icing sugar.

Heat a skewer in a flame until it is red-hot. Use it to create diagonal lines on four of the pastry sheets.

To prepare the vanilla crème patisserie, combine the milk, sugar and vanilla pod in a saucepan and bring to the boil. Remove the mixture from the heat and add the flour and egg yolks. Return the crème patisserie to a low heat and cook for approximately 5 minutes until it becomes thick. Refrigerate until needed.

Make the raspberry coulis by bringing the raspberries, sugar and water to the boil. Lower the temperature and simmer until a pouring consistency is reached. Strain the mixture through a sieve and set aside to cool.

When ready to serve, arrange alternate layers of pastry and of crème patisserie and fresh berries on a serving plate, finishing with the bar-marked pastry sheet. Reserve some of the berries.

Garnish with remaining berries, raspberry coulis and fresh mint.

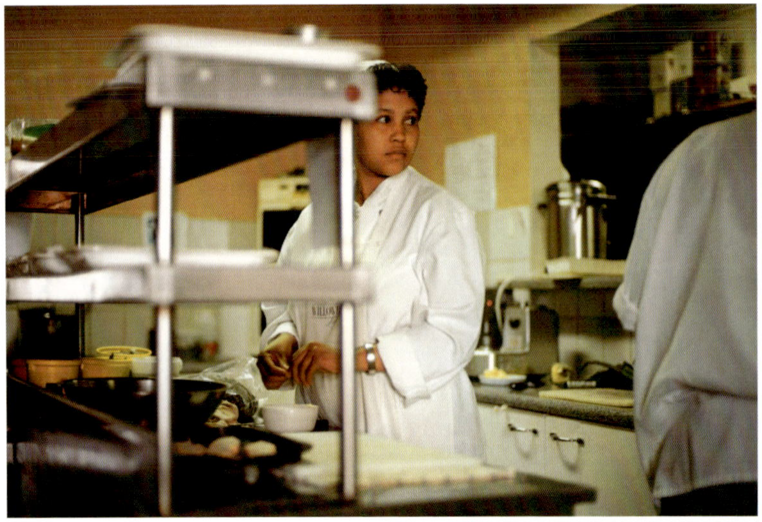
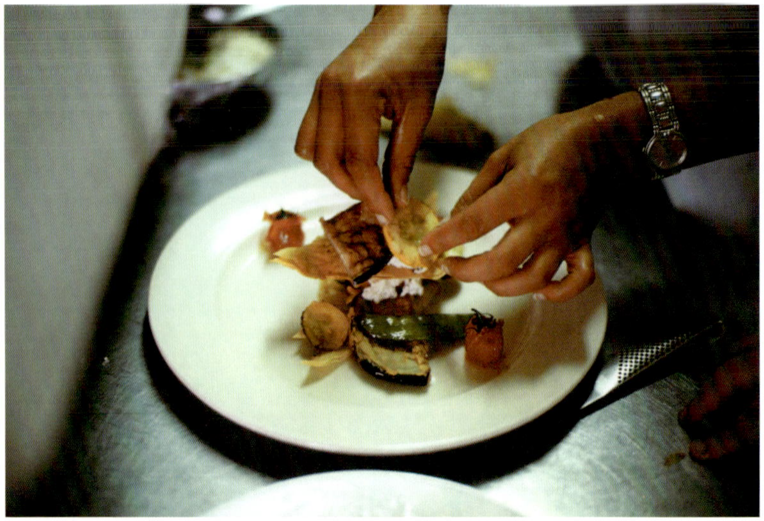
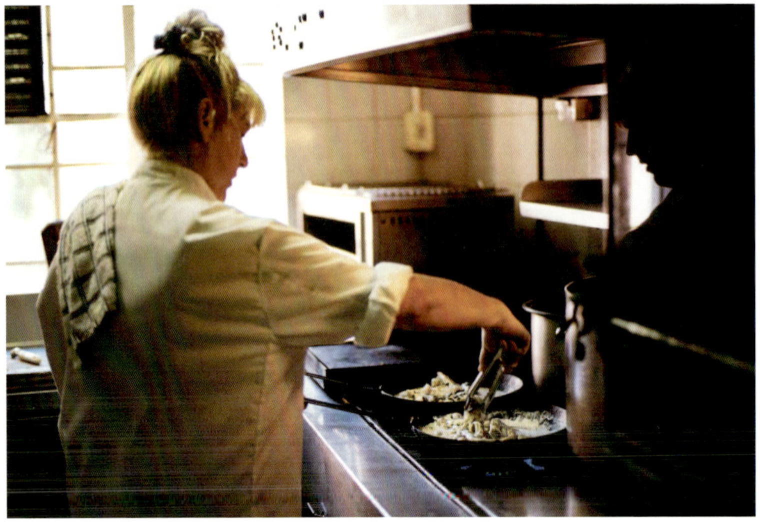
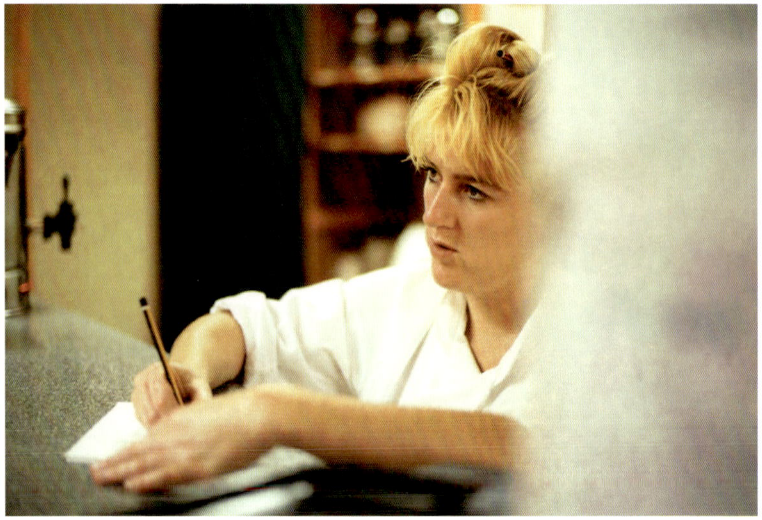

Glossary

Chargrilled

Grilling vegetables in a griddle pan until griddle lines are noticeable. Do not heat oil in the pan. Rather rub the oil on the vegetables. This will make the griddle lines more noticeable.

Coulis

The cooking together of fruit, sugar and water until an appropriate thickness is reached for the mixture to be used as a sauce on the plate.

Flambé

The addition of alcohol to a hot pan and igniting it to cause the alcohol to evaporate.

Fondant mould

A cylindrical, bottomless mould, 6 cm in diameter and 6 cm deep, used to produce dishes, usually desserts, where the outside and top is set, but the centre is still liquid.

Petit farcis

Baby seasonal vegetables, hollowed out and filled with a variety of fillings.

Ramekin

A small dish, 8–10 cm in diameter and 3–5cm high, that resembles a soufflé dish. Ramekins are usually made of ovenproof china or glass.

Reduce

To thicken a liquid by boiling it rapidly. The water is evaporated, thereby reducing the volume and intensifying the flavour. The sauce is considered thick when it coats the back of a spoon and does not run off.

Sauté

To cook meat, fish or vegetables in small amount of fat or oil until brown.

Tapenade

A condiment made with capers, desalted anchovies and pitted olives, pounded in a mortar and seasoned with olive oil, lemon juice and black pepper.

Vegetable terrine

Vegetables layered and pressed into a mould or other fairly deep container and set with gelatine, therefore making it easier to cut into slices when turned out.

Timbale

Alternating layers of various foodstuffs.

Zest

The brightly coloured, thin outer skin of citrus fruits, which is full of flavourful oils.

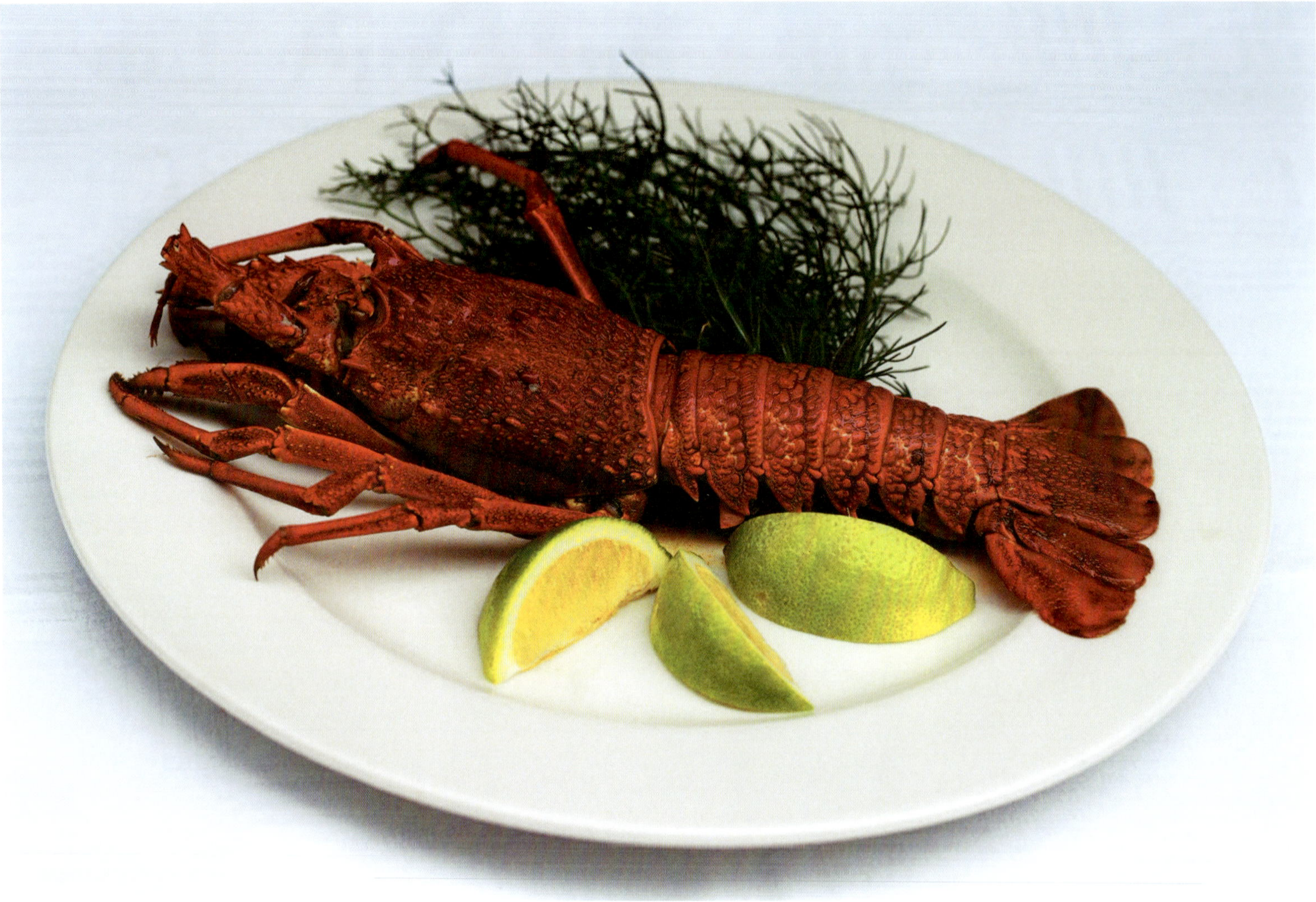

Index

apple and fig: samoosas 98, *99*
aubergine: caviar *32*, 33; salsa 26, *27*; timbale *32*, 33

basil pesto 40, *41*
beef, fillet of *70*, 71
beetroot: carpaccio (with kudu) *28*, 29; chips 30, *31*; galette 30, *31*; sauce 30, *31*; soup *24*, 25
Bekker, Anton 15–16, *16*, *19*
berries: coulis 82, *83*; mille feuille *104*, 105; minted *92*, 93; raspberry vinaigrette *28*, 29; strawberries (minted) *64*, 65
berry coulis 82, *83*
bisque sauce 60, *61*
broccoli soup *24*, 25
brûlée, crème *100*, 101

cake: Mames (chocolate) 88, *89*; sweet potato 96, *97*
Camembert cheese 52, *53*
carpaccio, beetroot and kudu *28*, 29
caviar: aubergine *32*, 33
chargrilled (def.) 107
cheese: Camembert 52, *53*; goat (galette) 30, *31*; Parmesan tuile 76, *77*; Stilton, with grilled pears 94, *95*
chicken: Thai green *62*, 63
chickpea chips *54*, 54–55
chive mashed potato 58, *59*
chocolate: cake 88, *89*; fondant 86, *87*; mousse 90, *91*; ravioli 90, *91*; sauce 102, *103*
coulis: berry 82, *83*; def. 107; raspberry *104*, 105; red pepper *40*, 41
couscous 60, *61*
crème patisserie: orange *80*, 81; vanilla *104*, 105

crêpe: soufflé *80*, 81; wild mushroom *36*, 37
crusts: marrow *70*, 71; pistachio 66, *67*; tomato and onion 54, 54–55

desserts 79–105
Drambuie ganache 96, *97*
duck: liver parcels *74*, 75; risotto 76, *77*

fennel bulbs, poached 58, *59*
fig: samoosas (with apple) 98, *99*
fish 56, *57*: cakes (Thai) 46, *47*; filling (ravioli) *44*, 45; linefish *54*, 54–55; petit farcis 56, *57*; sauce 58, *59*; smoked salmon 26, *27*; stock 58–59
fishcakes: Thai 46, *47*
flambé (def.) 107
fondant: hot chocolate 86, *87*; mould (def.) 107

galette: beetroot, goat cheese and walnut 30, 31
game: kudu *28*, 29, 72, *73*; ostrich 42, *43*, 66, *67*; springbok *64*, 65
ganache: Drambuie 96, *97*

honey and rosemary sauce *70*, 71

jus, redcurrant 72, *73*

kudu: carpaccio *28*, 29; medallions 72, *73*

leeks: and potato soup *24*, 25; deep-fried julienne *70*, 71
lemon curd 82, *83*
lentils: salad 38, *39*
linefish, *see* fish
Livesey, Loran 9, *14*, 14, 15–16, *16*, 50, 107

main meals 49–77
marrow crust *70*, 71
Marsala sauce 68, *69*
mayonnaise 42, *43*
Mbana, Pearl *16*, *19*
meringues, hazelnut 82, *83*

mille feuille: berry *104*, 105; vegetable *40*, 41, 72, *73*
minted berries *92*, 93
mousse: chocolate 90, *91*
mushrooms 56, *57*: crêpe *36*, 37; sauce 52, *53*; wild *36*, 37

Norwegian salmon 58, 59
nuts: hazelnut meringue 82, *83*; macadamia (kudu) 72, *73*; pecan nut pie *84*, 85; pistachio crust (ostrich) 66, *67*; walnuts (beetroot galette) 30, *31*

onions 68, *69*
orange: crème patisserie *80*, 81; crêpe soufflé *80*, 81; duck *74*, 75; sauce *74*, 75
ostrich: medallions 66, *67*; tartare 42, *43*
oysters: tempura *54*, 55

parfait: minted berry *92*, 93
Parmesan cheese tuile 76, *77*
pasta: chocolate ravioli 90, *91*; homemade *44*, 45, 90, *91*; seafood ravioli *44*, 45; tagliatelle 68, *69*
pastry: crème patisserie *80*, 81; *104*, 105; pie crust *84*, 85; puff 34, *35*; samoosas (fig and apple) 98, *99*
Pearce, Ed 15–16, *16*, *19*
pears: grilled with Stilton cheese 94, *95*
pecan nuts: pie *84*, 85
pesto: basil *40*, 41; coriander 60
petit farcis 56, *57*; def. 107
pie: pecan nut *84*, 85
pistachio nuts: ostrich 66, 67
polenta 56, *57*
potato: and leek soup *24*, 25; galettes 66, *67*; gratin 72, *73*; mashed (chive) 58, *59*
prawns 60, *61*; curry *62*, 63
puff pastry sticks 34, *35*
pulses: chickpea chips *54*, 54–55; lentil salad 38, *39*

ramekin (def.) 107

raspberry: coulis *104*, 105; vinaigrette *28*, 29
ratatouille 56, *57*
ravioli: chocolate 90, *91*; seafood *44*, 45
red pepper coulis *40*, 41
redcurrant sauce *72*, 73
reduce (def.) 107
risotto: duck and pumpkin 76, *77*
rosemary and honey sauce *70*, 71
rösti: Camembert, smoked salmon and mushroom sauce 52, *53*

saffron sauce 54, 54–55
salad: lentils 38, *39*
salmon: Norwegian 58, *59*; smoked *26*, 27, 52, *53*
salsa: aubergine *26*, 27
samoosas: fig and apple 98, *99*
sauce: bisque 60, *61*; chocolate 102, *103*; fish 58, *59*; Marsala 68, *69*; mushroom 52, *53*; orange 74, *75*; redcurrant jus *72*, 73; rosemary and honey *70*, 71; saffron 54, 54–55; seafood 60, *61*
sauté (def.) 107
seafood: oysters 54, 54–55; prawns 60, *61*, *62*, 63; ravioli *44*, 45
smoked salmon *26*, 27, 52, *53*: home smoking 26
Smoked Salmon and Aubergine Salsa *26*, 27
soufflé: orange crêpe *80*, 81
soups: beetroot *24*, 25; broccoli *24*, 25; leek and potato *24*, 25
spatzle 64, *65*
springbok fillets 64, *65*
starters 23–47
Stilton cheese: with grilled pears 94, *95*
strawberries: hot minted 64, *65*
sweet potato: cake 96, *97*; chips 96, *97*

tapenade (def.) 107
tartare: ostrich 42, *43*
tempura oysters 54, 55
terrine vegetable 34, *35*
Thai: fishcakes 46, *47*; green chicken *62*, 63
timbale: aubergine *32*, 33; def. 107

tomato and cumin crust 54, *55*
tuiles: savoury (Parmesan) 76, *77*; sweet 102, *103*
vanilla crème patisserie *104*, 105
veal medallions 68, *69*
vegetables: aubergine salsa *26*, 27; aubergine timbale *32*, 33; beetroot and kudu carpaccio *28*, 29; beetroot chips 30, *31*; beetroot galette 30, *31*; mille feuille *40*, 41, *72*, 73; petit farcis 56, *57*; pumpkin and duck risotto 76, *77*; ratatouille 56, *57*; terrine 34, *35*, (def.) 107; soups *24*, 25; wild mushrooms filling *36*, 37 (*see also* potato)
vinaigrette, raspberry *28*, 29

wild mushrooms: crêpe *36*, 37

zest (def.) 107

Index of Recipes

Beetroot and Kudu Carpaccio with Raspberry Vinaigrette *28*, 29
Beetroot, Goat Cheese and Walnut Galette 30, *31*
Berry Mille Feuille *104*, 105
Black Pepper-crusted Springbok with Hot Minted Strawberries and Spatzle 64, *65*

Chocolate Ravioli 90, *91*
Crème Brûlée *100*, 101
Creole Sweet Potato Cake 96, *97*

Duck and Pumpkin Risotto 76, *77*

Fig and Apple Samoosas 98, *99*
Fillet of Beef with Marrow Crust, Rosemary and Honey Sauce and Julienne Leeks *70*, 71
Fish Petit Farcis 56, *57*

Grilled Pears with Stilton Cheese 94, *95*

Hot Chocolate Fondant 86, *87*
Hot Minted Berry Parfait 92, *93*

Kudu Medallions Rolled in Nuts with Redcurrant Jus and Potato Gratin *72*, 73

Layered Hazelnut Meringues with Berry Coulis 82, *83*
Lentil Salad with Lettuce 38, *39*
Linefish Chermoula with Tempura Oysters, Chickpea Chips and Saffron Sauce 54, 54–55

Mames Cake 88, *89*

Orange Crêpe Soufflé *80*, 81
Orange Duck Magret with Duck Liver Parcels 74, *75*
Ostrich Tartare 42, *43*

Pecan Nut Pie 84, *85*
Pistachio-crusted Ostrich Medallions with Potato Galettes 66, *67*

Seafood Ravioli *44*, 45
Seed-crusted Norwegian Salmon with Poached Fennel Bulbs and Chive Mashed Potato 58, *59*

Thai Green Chicken and Prawn Curry *62*, 63
Tiger Prawns with Couscous and Bisque Sauce 60, *61*

Timbale of Aubergine *32*, 33
Tiramisu 102, *103*
Trio of Rösti 52, *53*
Trio of Soup *24*, 25

Veal Medallions with Tagliatelle, Onions and Marsala Sauce 68, *69*
Vegetable Mille Feuille with Basil Pesto and Red Pepper Coulis *40*, 41
Vegetable Terrine 34, *35*

Wild Mushroom Crêpe *36*, 37
Willowbrook Thai Fishcakes 46, *47*

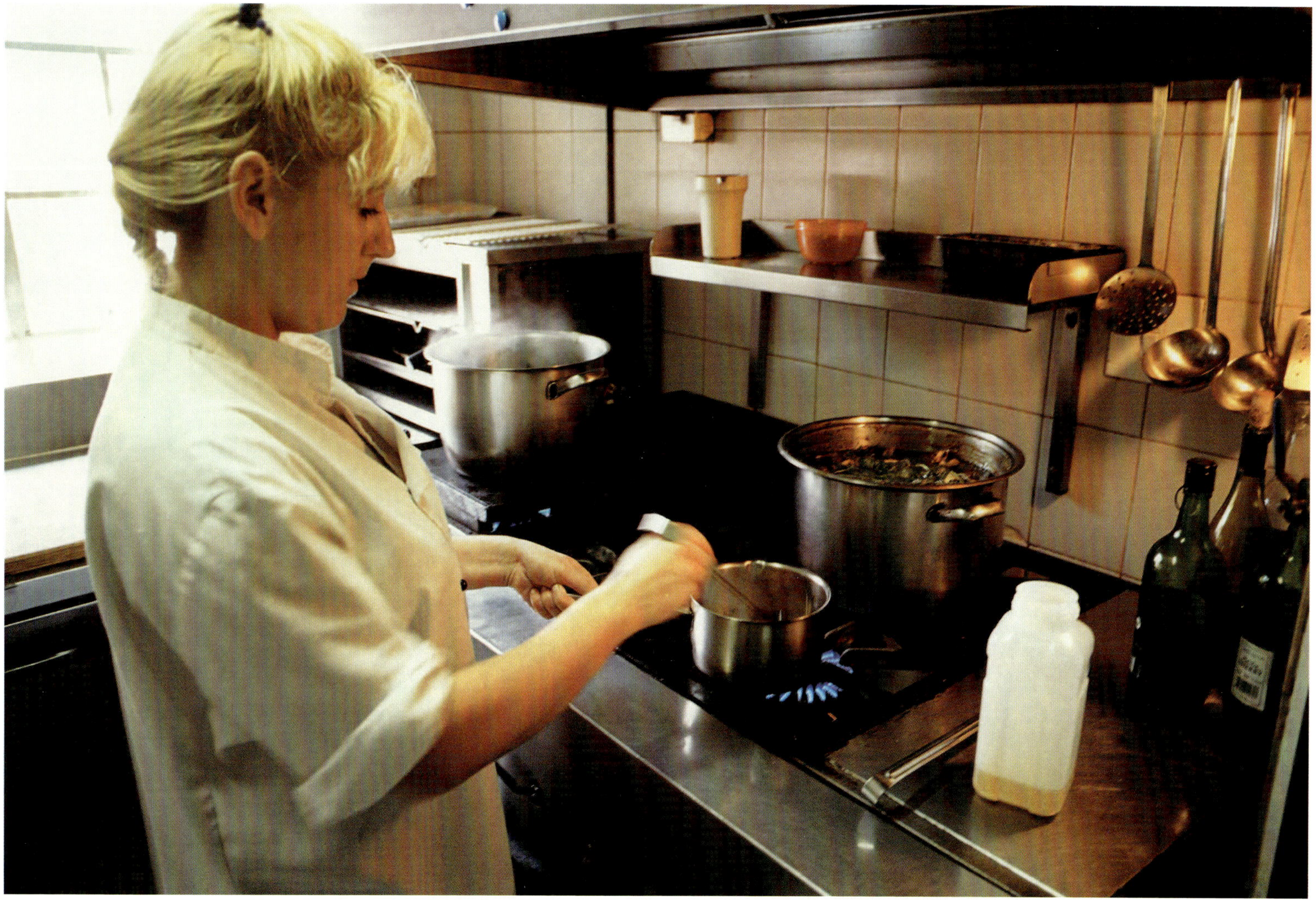

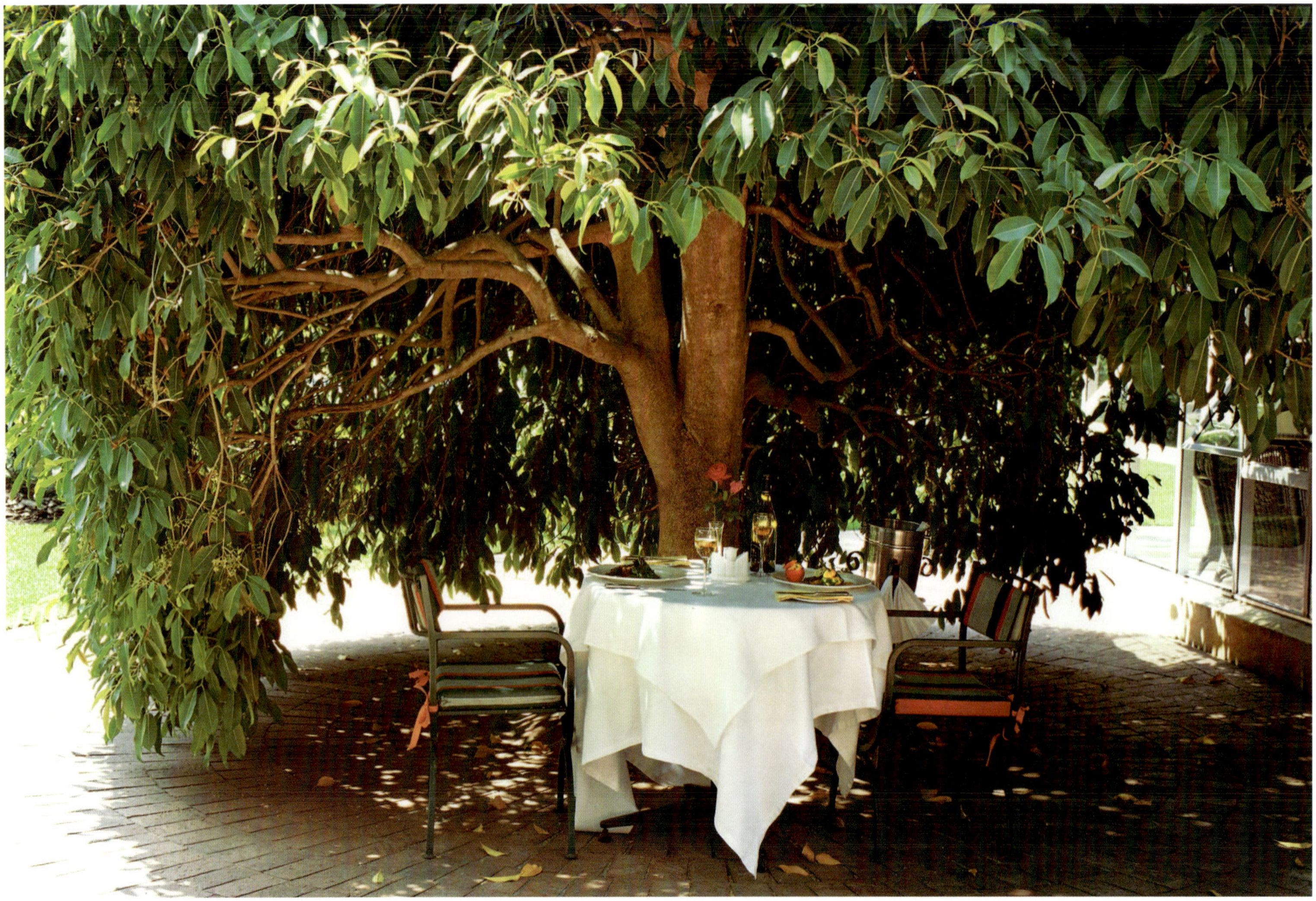

DATE/DATUM	NAME/NAAM	ADDRESS/ADRES	Comments
7/12/02	Bleyenbergh Jef + Julie	Hoofdstraat 45 St. Jansteen - Hulst Holland - 4564 AM	we will come back!
8/12/02	MAGGIE JACQUELINE	COLEMANS HATCH EAST SUSSEX	A LITTLE PIECE OF HEAVEN ON EARTH - BE BACK SOON.
10.12.02	Helga + Albert Bender	Hermannstr. 11 64380 Erlausen	Beautiful house + service
11/12/02	Adrian & Mary Murphy	DALKEY, Co. Dublin IRELAND	Great to be BACK!
13/12/02	Angelika Michael Katharina	Germany	best crème brûlée of the region loved it.
22/12/02	Enrico & Chantal	Lugano (TI) Switzerland	Ostrich tartare DELICIOUS
25/12/02	Kees Wijnten Loes Smit	Nederland (Zandhaagse 5a Heyland)	Third time. Still great!
31.12.02	Gaby Schio Paul Trunz	Wettingen / Zürich Switzerland	Thank you all, it was a wonderful place.